THE SECRET OF ALIGNMENT

Unleash the Power of Attunement in Your Life

SIRSHREE

THE SECRET OF ALIGNMENT

Unleash the Power of Attunement in Your Life
By **Sirshree** Tejparkhi

Copyright © Tejgyan Global Foundation
All Rights Reserved 2023

Tejgyan Global Foundation is a charitable organization with its headquarters in Pune, India.

ISBN : 978-93-90607-67-9

Published by WOW Publishings Pvt. Ltd., India
First Edition published in May 2023

Printed and bound by Trinity Academy, Pune, INDIA

This book is the translation of the Hindi book titled
"Power of Tuning-Secret of Alignment" by Sirshree Tejparkhi.

Copyright and publishing rights are vested exclusively with WOW Publishings Pvt. Ltd. This book is sold subject to the condition that it shall not by way of trade or otherwise, be lent, resold, hired out, or otherwise circulated without the publisher's prior written consent in any form of binding or cover other than that in which it is published and without a similar condition including this condition being imposed on the subsequent purchaser and without limiting the rights under copyright reserved above, no part of this publication may be reproduced, stored in or introduced into a retrieval system, or transmitted, in any form, or by any means, electronic, mechanical, photocopying, recording or otherwise, without the prior written permission of both the copyright owner and the above-mentioned publisher of this book. Any person who does any unauthorized act in relation to this publication may be liable to criminal prosecution and civil claims for damages.

Although the author and publisher have made every effort to ensure accuracy of content in this book, they hereby disclaim any liability to any party for any loss, damage, or disruption caused by errors or omissions, resulting from negligence, accident, or any other cause. Readers are advised to take full responsibility to exercise discretion in understanding and applying the content of this book.

To,
the divine providence of nature
in the form of its flora and fauna
that live in harmony with one another,
and in alignment with the laws of nature.

Contents

Preface		7
Introduction 1 - How to Recognize the Divine Vibration		9
Introduction 2 - What to Do If the Mind is Negative		13
SECTION 1 - Introducing The Power of Alignment		**17**
1.	With Whom to Align	19
2.	The Conflicts of Being In-tune and Out-of-tune	24
3.	Own the Responsibility for Your Mistuning	30
4.	The First Step to Improve One's Tuning	36
SECTION 2 - Aligning With the External World		**43**
5.	Harmonious Tuning in Relationships	45
6.	Release the Reins and Get Attuned	51
7.	Attain Better Tuning with Completeness	56
8.	Alignment Changes with The Company You Keep	61
9.	Effect of Change on Alignment	66
SECTION 3 - Aligning With Your Inner World		**75**
10.	Autosuggestions for Attunement	77
11.	Effect of Feelings on Our Alignment	84
12.	Mind Your Emotions, Master Your Life	90

13.	Ask Pivotal Questions to Get Aligned	95
14.	The Story that Disrupts Your Alignment	102
15.	The Alignment of the Body, Mind, and Intellect	107

SECTION 4 - Aligning With Your True Nature — 113

16.	God Also Seeks Mutual Alignment	115
17.	Be in the Feeling of Havingness	121
18.	An Impersonal Life Boosts the Melody in Alignment	126
19.	Fine Tuning with Divine Love	133
20.	The Art of Staying Aligned	138
	Appendix	147-152

Note:

In this book, terms like "Divine attunement", "Alignment with the divine tune", "Tuning with God", and "Alignment with nature" are used in various contexts. But they all essentially mean the same—being in the feeling of happiness by getting rid of the disturbance of the mind. This is the law of free flow.

A few topics have been repeated intentionally to ensure a complete, thorough understanding of the imperceptible details.

Preface

Attunement Is Essentially Free Flow

The human mind and body are intimately connected. There is a proverb, "As is the mind, so is the body." We can extend this further and say, "As is the mind, so is the body, and so is our life." Our entire life is a reflection of our mind. The state of our mind determines whether we live a happy or sad life, a peaceful or chaotic one.

One of the facets of the human mind often remains in a state of contrast and duality. It sways between happiness and sorrow, pride and shame, love and hate, good and bad. The mind also has an intuitive aspect that allows us to flow freely.

Nature operates in harmony. Flora and fauna blossom according to nature's divine programming. In contrast, humans struggle with many physical and mental problems. Life is becoming more difficult and chaotic. Anxiety, depression, disappointment, and suicidal thoughts are becoming common problems. These problems were unheard of before. Despite technological advancements and facilities, man seems to be steeped in conflict and suffering, even though he has everything.

Alignment is the key to a happy and harmonious life. Every relationship, be it with society, family, colleagues, subordinates, bosses, or nature, requires alignment for harmony.

Consider the life of a husband and wife. Both may have totally different personalities. Their likes, dislikes, habits, and mindsets could differ from one another. And yet, if they have good coordination and tuning, they can live happily and help each other grow. But they can become a misfortune for each other if they lack alignment with each other.

Alignment begins by attuning with our Self within. The Self is also called the Source, God, Divine nature, or Consciousness. Once we connect with our Self, external things fall into place. This is the secret of alignment, the essence of free flow.

This tuning, that God has planned and programmed for everyone, works in everyone's life naturally. The knowledge that rightly sets this divine alignment in motion is called "Law of Alignment." It is the attunement of life with the divine nature or grace. When we are in tune with our divine nature, whatever we desire starts flowing into our life effortlessly.

This book serves as a guide to attune to this divine vibration and regain the lost alignment in our lives. We will learn whom we must align with, how to align, what disturbs this alignment, how to correct it, and how to lead a successful, happy, prosperous, powerful, effective, and meaningful life by setting our alignment.

Let us harmonize with this unique design of nature, follow the law of alignment, and see what wonders it can bring into our lives.

Introduction 1

How to Recognize the Divine Vibration

Have you ever wondered why Hindus ring the bell when entering a temple, why an artist bows down before performing, or why people worship their factories, vehicles, gadgets, account books, and homes during the Hindu festival Dusshera? All of these actions are meant to align with the divine vibration.

Have you ever pondered on how you discern whether you are experiencing joy or sorrow? Have you ever asked yourself, "How do I sense the emotional turmoil within me? Does anyone report it from the outside, or do I feel it within?"

Our emotions convey whether we are content or discontent, calm or agitated. They notify us whether we are in alignment with the divine vibration. When we are unhappy, distressed, irritable, angry, revengeful, fearful, or anxious for no apparent reason, it is an indication that we have lost our tuning with the divine vibration.

Today, Science has also proven that the entire universe is resonating at a frequency. Pictures of this phenomenon are also available. In nature, everything operates rhythmically. If we are in tune, no one will have any complaints or bad feelings about each other, and everything will happen beautifully in a well-defined manner.

Let us understand this with the example of a radio. A radio has various stations that are tuned to different frequencies. If we want to listen to a song from a particular station, we have to tune our radio to the exact frequency of that station, neither less nor more. Otherwise, we will hear a lot of disturbing noise.

Similarly, we need to tune in with nature, God, or the divine vibration. If our tuning is disturbed, we will experience turmoil and noise within. However, when we are in harmony with nature, we will experience the same melodious song, happiness, wonder, appreciation, love, peace, tranquility, and satisfaction that exists in nature. It is like tuning our inner radio to the right frequency to enjoy the symphony of life fully.

On this basis, whenever we feel sad, it indicates that we are not in alignment with the divine vibration. When we feel happy, it suggests that we are in alignment with the divine vibration. Staying in harmony with the divine vibration leads to fulfilling all our good intentions that benefit all and cause no harm. With alignment, we attract the solutions we seek, and things start flowing smoothly into our life. When we fall out of alignment, it may create obstacles that block our progress.

For example, if someone is experiencing problems in their marriage, health, or finances, it is the result of their misalignment with the divine vibration. If they work on bringing back their alignment with the divine vibration, their problems will soon begin to get resolved.

Consider the famous snake boat race in Kerala, which illustrates the importance of teamwork and the symphony of natural forces. Winning the race requires all team members to harmonize with each other, working towards the same goal. The boat moves swiftly toward its destination when all the rowers paddle together with the same rhythm and intensity. Any disharmony among the rowers can prevent the boat from reaching its destination. The race teaches us

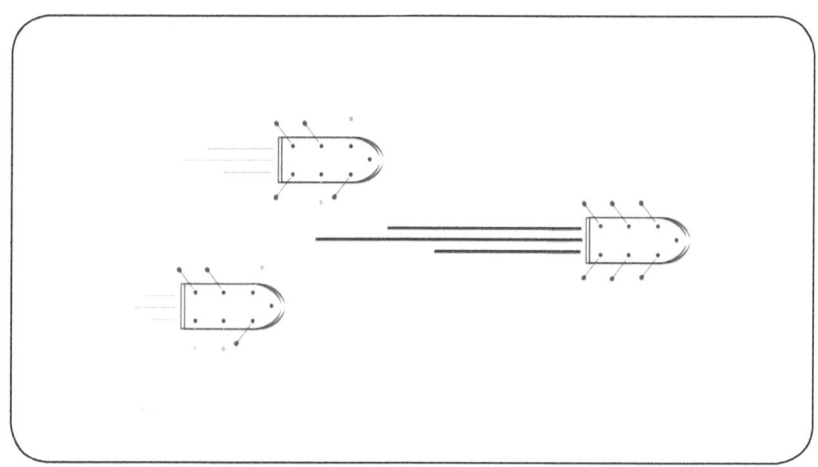

the importance of being in tune with each other and with nature. Aligning with the divine vibration and being in sync with others can help us easily achieve our goals.

To determine whether we are attuned to nature, we can ask ourselves the following question several times a day: "Am I aligned with the divine vibration? Am I in love with the divine vibration?" If we receive a positive answer, we should celebrate. This practice will help us attune to the natural rhythm of the universe and enhance our happiness.

On the other hand, if we are not aligned with the divine vibration, we need to take responsibility for realigning with nature.

When all our body parts work in harmony with each other, we feel healthy. Even if one body part is unwell, our body falls sick. It loses harmony with the rest of the body parts. In such a situation, the diseased body parts have to be cured to regain health. We need to follow a nutritious diet and exercise besides taking the required medications.

Similarly, if we lose the tuning with nature, we must take responsibility. No one else can do it for us. We need to take steps to bring back our alignment. Whenever we are not in alignment with the divine vibration, we need to immediately shift our frequency to the happiness state. When we feel happy, we start attuning to the divine vibration.

Consider how a musical orchestra works. Multiple musical instruments are played together in harmony to create beautiful melodies. If any of them falls out of alignment, the music sounds chaotic. Similarly, when we are aligned with nature, we start experiencing the melodious music of divine happiness playing within us.

Everything is abundant in nature, and nature wants to give abundantly to everyone. We just need to guide our focus and feelings toward positivity. This will align us with the natural rhythm of the universe.

Introduction 2

What to Do If the Mind is Negative

So far, we have learned about the divine vibration and its importance. However, sometimes our mind may still be filled with distracting thoughts. In such moments, we can use the following steps to realign our mind.

Step 1: The first step to change the tuning of our mind is to practice breathing meditation. To begin, it is essential to carefully read and understand the instructions before closing your eyes to start the meditation. Let us take a closer look at this step.

- Assume a meditation posture or the posture of your choice.

- Close your eyes and concentrate on your breath as you inhale and exhale.

- As you begin breathing in a slow rhythm, ask yourself, "Am I aligned with the divine vibration?" Then, focus on your emotions and feel them.

- If you are feeling happy, know that you are in sync with the divine vibration.

- If you are feeling peaceful, know that you are in love with the divine vibration.

- If you are not feeling good, focus on your breath again.

- After a while, slowly open your eyes and observe how you feel now.

- Your feelings are the only indicators to know whether you are attuned. There is no other way to know it.

Step 2: Recall the blessings that have been showered upon you. We have been fortunate to receive so many things, such as a healthy body, the gift of breath, a lovely home, and loving relationships. We can remind ourselves of these blessings to help us align with the divine vibration.

Step 3: Delve deep into your blessings and write them down in a gratitude journal. Acknowledge even the smallest of the blessings showered upon you. Write down at least one blessing every night before going to bed. You will soon realize how abundant your life is and how fortunate you are to have these blessings. Keep reading the journal from time to time to feel the magic of gratitude. Just by remembering these blessings, your feelings change, and you become attuned to the divine vibration of nature.

Step 4: Whenever your mind fills with negativity, close your eyes, and visualize divine white light beaming from the Universe showering on you. Imagine this white light being showered on the entire universe, Earth, your country, city, street, home, and finally, your body. As your whole body basks in this white light, your feelings and emotions align with the divine vibration.

Step 5: When your mind is filled with negativity, avoid exposing yourself to media that triggers negative or fearful thoughts. Instead, choose to watch some lighthearted programs that lift your spirit, listen to pleasant music, participate in a sport, engage in a hobby, spend time in nature's beautiful landscapes, or do something that makes you happy. These positive activities will surely help you attune to the divine vibration of nature.

The goal of these practices is to align with the divine vibration. Those who are committed to this goal will find ways to achieve it. To do this, it is crucial to take responsibility for your emotions and strive to be happy throughout the day.

Now that we have understood the importance of aligning with nature using the above steps, let us explore the power of aligning with the divine vibration in the following chapters.

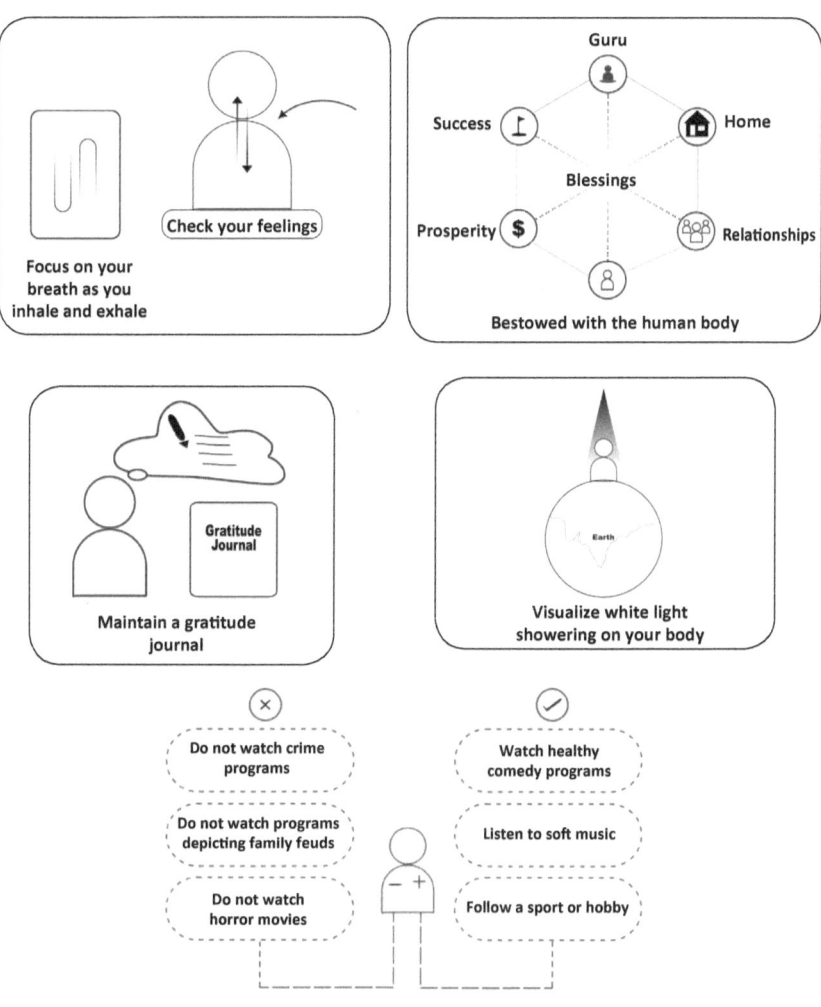

SECTION - 1

Introducing The Power of Alignment

1

With Whom to Align

Far beyond the sky, there was a wonderland of music where a solo flute played sweet melodies. The melodies were so captivating that they affected everyone far and wide. All who heard it would be immersed in eternal joy and peace. Birds would chirp happily; trees and plants would swirl and dance joyfully. The moon, stars, clouds, and breeze followed its rhythm as they traversed their path. The solo flute reigned that music land.

One day, the flute thought, "How nice it would be if some other companion instruments produced various tunes along with mine! If they all get tuned to my melody, how joyous it would be! Such a melodious orchestra can fill the entire atmosphere with its wonderful sound. The entire cosmos would eternally resonate with the divine rhythm."

With this thought, the flute played such divine music that many musical instruments, like the guitar, harmonium, sitar, violin, drum, and more, emerged with their own unique power. These instruments came into existence to render melodious music. They instinctively began playing music according to their nature. Their music was well in-tune with the flute. Their combined melody seemed like a celebration in the entire universe. All flora and fauna enjoyed the divine music and lived with joy, wonder, and appreciation.

In the beginning, the musical instruments were fully aware that the flute had created them and attuned to the flute's tune. But gradually, they lost this awareness. Every instrument considered itself different and superior to the others. Instead of focusing on the quality of the combined orchestrated melody, they now focused on their solo tune. They thought, "Let my tune be better than others. Let it be more heard, recognized, appreciated, and respected than the rest."

As a result, they fell out of tune with the flute. They began playing louder to suppress the tunes of the other instruments, thus disturbing their synergy. The melodious and joyous music became chaotic, disturbing the entire universe. The musical instruments that were "in-tune" became "out-of-tune," and no one wanted to listen to their music anymore.

When does music become noisy?

Despite the immense talent and capability of the musical instruments, their once beautiful symphony became chaotic because they fell out of sync. Their alignment got disturbed. This emphasizes the importance of alignment as a quality that can elevate even an ordinary individual performance to the height of an extraordinary orchestra.

This story of the flute and musical instruments is our own story, represented by different symbols. The flute that emits music ceaselessly represents the divine vibration, the universal tune, the Source, God, Consciousness, or Self. The source is that origin from where the divine vibration of life is transmitted to the entire universe. The source manifests divine qualities such as love, joy, peace, abundance, perfect health, contentment, and devotion evenly at all places and at all times.

In the previous example, the flute depicts God. The other musical instruments represent human beings. God created human beings so that He could express and admire His qualities and experience Himself to the fullest through human bodies. Human beings remembered God's intention for a very long time. Our ancestors lived a simple life by being aligned with the Source. But people have gradually started losing this understanding in the modern era. Their perspective has become more personal and limited. They have become self-centered. Instead of benevolently thinking, "May everyone be blessed. May everyone progress," they are consumed by narrow-minded thoughts, like "Let me benefit first. I must shine like a unique star."

Today, the entire universe, the flora and fauna, operate and live happily in alignment with the divine vibration. But human beings alone live out of sync with the divine vibration due to their beliefs.

All human beings are born in a natural or default alignment with the divine vibration. But, as we grow up, seeing people of lowered consciousness around us and staying in their company, we also start becoming like them. After meeting with disruptive experiences, our pure mind gets polluted with disorders like deceit, ego, jealousy, hatred, depression, sorrow, and ambition, leading to misalignment with the divine vibration.

As we lose our alignment with the divine vibration, we pay the price in the form of sorrow, incompleteness, dissatisfaction, failure, ailments, ignorance, and so on. We forget that our happiness and contentment are not dependent on external factors but on our fine-tuning with God and the divine vibration.

If we are able to bring back our alignment with the divine vibration in some way, we can break free of all problems in our life. Then we do not need to look for external reasons to be happy. We can remain happy and content without any reason just by reveling in divine alignment. Our life can become an expression of unconditional joy instead of suffering.

The principle of free flow

Understanding and applying the principle of free flow helps us achieve this fine-tuning with the divine vibration. It teaches us how to align with nature and attune to the divine vibration to live a simple, easy, and successful life. It helps us achieve our ultimate goal.

The principle of free flow needs us to shift from head to heart. When we attain the right understanding of our intuitive mind, we become free from the ego and stabilize in the Self. Our life becomes filled with bliss and peace.

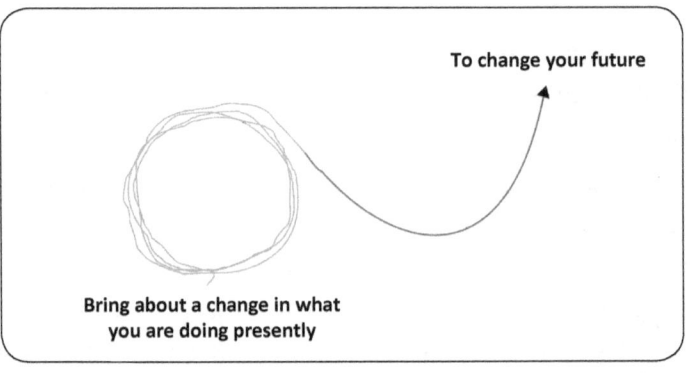

When we notice that we are not aligned with nature, or when we feel disturbed, sorrowful, irritated, rejected, or distressed due to some unfulfilled desire, we need to understand the principle of free flow and bring it into practice. This will change our mistuning and fine-tune us with nature. Gradually, we will attune to the divine vibration, and one day we will emit the same divine melody as the Source.

In the forthcoming chapters, we will learn the art of attuning to the divine vibration.

Action plan:

1. Contemplate, do you ever experience incompleteness or dissatisfaction? If yes, why?
2. Set aside a few minutes for yourself every day and observe when you are out of tune with nature, i.e., notice when you are overwhelmed with irritation, depression, anger, or fear.
3. When you lose your alignment, immediately become aware and tell yourself, "There is nothing to worry about. I have just got mistuned. I only need to get it back."

The Conflicts of Being In-tune and Out-of-tune

Once, a musician visited an exhibition of antique musical instruments and found an old guitar with twice the number of strings of a regular guitar. It was a beautiful and exceptional guitar. The musician was very excited to purchase it at any cost.

The owner warned him, "I can sell the guitar, but beware, it is a very strange guitar. While some of its strings create tunes that give immense joy, some other strings can cause intense pain. Also, there is another special thing about it. We cannot stop ourselves from playing it whenever we see it. So, in a way, it is a problem. It is like buying trouble. We will constantly keep swinging between happiness and sorrow. I am warning you in advance because it has made my life miserable."

After hearing this, the musician said confidently, "Don't worry about me; I can handle it. Just sell it to me." The owner sold the guitar to the musician. The musician happily brought it home.

Whenever the musician played the guitar, he would become either happy or sad. Gradually, he noticed that while plucking on some strings gladdened him, other strings saddened him. Now he tried to pluck only those strings that would make him happy.

Slowly, with consistent practice, he trained his fingers to pluck only the happiness strings. With this, he reveled in everlasting bliss and contentment.

Now, this is not merely a story. It is an analogy that points to the working of the human mind. The exceptional guitar represents our mind; its strings are our joyful and painful thoughts. We are always caught amid the conflict between these joyful and painful thoughts. Like the musician, we, too, need to avoid this conflict and attune ourselves to the divine vibration.

The mistuning demons of sorrow

You may have read the mythological stories of various demons. These demons would wreak havoc, causing grave suffering to people. Then the gods would gather all their forces to destroy them. These demons symbolize the thoughts that cause sorrow within us. The moment we deviate from the Source, our entire perspective of life changes. We, then, start plucking the wrong strings, thus creating wrong thoughts.

Wrong thoughts cause sorrow, irritation, and anger within us, even for the least trivial things. This happens when our consciousness shifts its focus away from the Source and gets consumed by our tendencies. This, in turn, gives rise to the demons of sorrowful thoughts that wreak havoc within us. This will stop only when we attune to the Source and pluck the right strings of happiness again. They will create the right tunes and the right thoughts. The moment we are in tune, the demons of sorrow will automatically disappear.

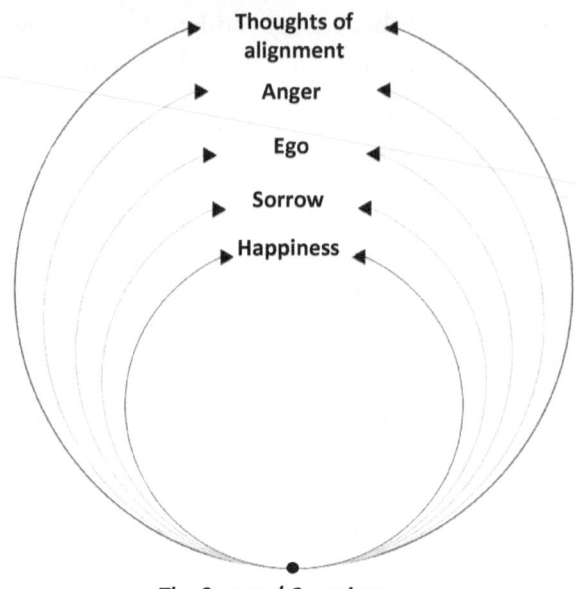

Every morning, when we wake up, our mental guitar starts playing. Many thoughts simultaneously flash into our mind, pertaining to housework, breakfast or lunch, office work, preparation for a meeting, etc. Sometimes, the thoughts are attuned to the Source; sometimes, they are not. When they are attuned, we are happy. When they are not attuned, we experience conflict, causing sorrow, irritation, and anger within us. Our mind continues to chatter, and we feel subdued within.

In the absence of free flow, we keep vacillating between the strings of demons and gods. Sometimes, we are in tune and sometimes out of tune; sometimes happy, sometimes unhappy. Let us understand how someone who is in tune can suddenly fall out of tune with an example.

Amar was an IT engineer. He had an important presentation with his client. Being efficient at work, he was confident that everything would work out in his favor. As soon as he woke up in the morning, positive thoughts arose in his mind, "Today's presentation is very crucial. If all goes well, our company will bag a big project. This will help me grow in my career," etc.

While thinking on these lines, he plucked the strings connected to the Source. But suddenly, he began thinking differently. "Yesterday, when Ashish was asked to get the projector, he said it was out for repairs and would be received only by the evening. What if the projector is not yet ready? And what if it has been received but stops working during my presentation? It will spoil my tempo in front of all the attendees. I have got my laptop ready, but the flash drive with the latest presentation file is with Aakash. He is a very forgetful person. What if he forgets to bring the flash drive? Often, he is not contactable on his phone. Oh God! What will happen now?" etc.

The moment the first negative thought flashed in his mind, he had plucked the strings of sorrow that were not connected to the Source but to the judgmental egoic mind. As these worrisome thoughts continued, he fell out of tune.

This is how our negative thoughts disturb our tuning with the divine vibration. Nothing changed in those five minutes except for the mistuning with the Source that led to the birth of the demons of sorrow.

How to be free of the demons of sorrow?

The demons of sorrow amplify and augment our anger, fear, anxiety, and many other tendencies within us. It is the biggest hurdle in our simple, straightforward, and powerful life. It is important to understand how to eliminate these demons.

We have been blessed with human life. Then, why not take its full advantage and attain the ultimate bliss by understanding the principle of free flow?

Understanding the principle of free flow makes our life easy and simple. It attunes us to the divine vibration and eliminates sorrow. When a voice touches our heart, it has no language and simply transcends all boundaries of religions and faiths. Similarly, with wisdom and understanding, when we align with nature, we become one with the universe. With this universal tune, the waves of happiness endlessly flow through our being. But we can relate to it and understand it only when we are attuned to the divine vibration.

To realign our tuning, first, we need to introspect honestly and assess when we are in tune and happy, and when we are out of tune or sad. We need to start this inquiry in the morning after waking up. We need to observe whether we are aligned with the Source; is this the same tune to which the birds chirp in unison, to which plants sway in harmony, and by which the sun rises relentlessly?

We need to experience that divine omnipresent harmony in which all the tunes of nature originate. This alignment will help us correct and bring back our alignment with the Source. In this immense peace, our pleasant feeling will let us know that we are attuned to nature and have become one with it.

Throughout the day, at regular intervals, we need to ask ourselves, "Am I aligned with the divine vibration at this moment?"

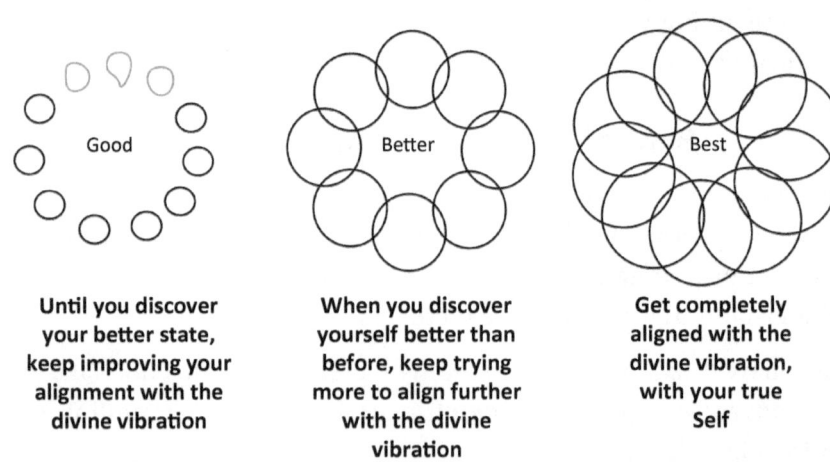

Until you discover your better state, keep improving your alignment with the divine vibration

When you discover yourself better than before, keep trying more to align further with the divine vibration

Get completely aligned with the divine vibration, with your true Self

We will get the answer to this question through our feelings. If we are experiencing negative thoughts or feelings of worry and distress, we are not aligned with the divine vibration. And if we are happy, peaceful, and enjoying our work, then we are attuned to the divine vibration. If we are out of tune, we need to apply the principle of free flow. We will understand it more in the subsequent chapters.

Action plan:

1. Set a reminder for some time and experience tuning with the divine vibration, i.e., love, joy, peace, and contentment within you. For that, repeatedly ask yourself, "Am I aligned with the divine vibration now?" If the answer is "Yes," be in the free flow and carry on with your daily activities in that flow. Repeat this question at least eight times a day.

2. If your alignment is missing, reflect on its reasons and note them down. Consider frequent causes such as thoughts about someone, anxiety about the future, or financial issues. Identifying these reasons and bringing them to light is the first step toward eliminating them.

Own the Responsibility for Your Mistuning

Many people often hold others responsible for disturbing their rhythm. They blame God, fate, or some external factor for their shortcomings or troubles.

For example, an employee might complain, "I can't succeed because I always get mean bosses." A daughter-in-law might grumble, "I would have been in tune if it was not for my mother-in-law." A husband may blame his wife for the lack of harmony in his life. A person with a short height may blame his father for those genes. A financially poor individual may curse God, "Had I been born into a rich family, everything would have been perfect. I would have inherited wealth like my friend."

Some blame their misalignment on Feng Shui, astrology, numerology, horoscopes, or other supernatural reasons. By doing so, they avoid taking responsibility for their sorrow and failures. They comfortably hide behind the curtain of excuses and keep brooding and complaining all their life.

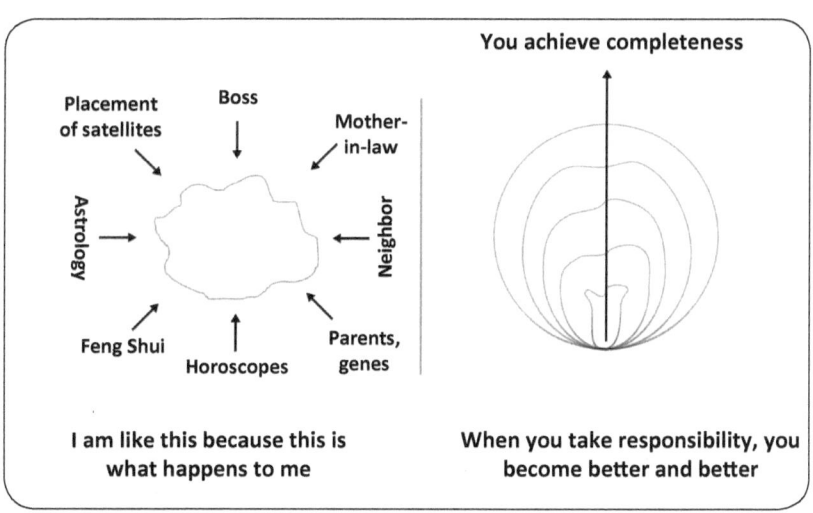

One needs to realize that the cause of all their sorrow and frustration is their very own actions arising out of ignorance. They can emerge from the abyss of their problems and misery only by addressing these actions and working on them. By doing so, they can take the right steps and correct their mistakes to prevent them from reoccurring. However, what happens to those who never see a fault in themselves? Well, they can never correct their alignment.

Understand the simple but powerful laws of life

Life on Earth operates according to the laws of nature. These laws are the same for everyone because Mother Nature never discriminates against or favors anyone. These laws are not based on an individual's designation, status, fame, caste, or religion. Instead, they are based on a simple formula: The seeds one sows, whether positive or negative, returns to them multi-fold.

Among all these laws of nature, the law of karma(actions) is the most important one. Everyone needs to understand this law, especially those who blame others for their plight and disown their responsibility.

Let us delve deeper into the law of karma. According to the principle of karma, we are solely responsible for our deeds and their consequences. No one else can receive the fruits of our deeds. In the same way, we never receive the fruits of others' deeds.

It is important to understand what constitutes karma. Karma encompasses not just our actions but also our intentions, feelings, thoughts, and speech. For example, if we think negatively about someone, it is our karma. If we feel angry at someone, it is again our karma. The words we speak and even our silence are karma because we consciously decide to be silent.

When one commits a wrong deed and a court case is filed against them, arguments, evidence, and witnesses are presented before the judge. The judge then delivers a verdict and punishes the offender. Sometimes, a criminal is acquitted due to the lack of evidence, and an innocent person is punished. However, in nature's court, such errors never happen. Nothing goes unnoticed; nature keeps an account of every thought and feeling, ensuring that its judgment is fair and just. Nature watches all our actions, records everything, and gives justice accordingly. Nature is ceaselessly at work.

The most important point is that the result of karma is not based on its external form but rather on the inner feeling and intention backing it. For example, if we tell lies for the well-being of someone, nature delivers the result for our intention of goodwill. Hence, despite having lied, we will receive a feeling of satisfaction and joy as a result from nature.

Your present action is your destiny

Many people blame their fate for everything and believe someone else is responsible for shaping their destiny. They consider themselves victims of conspiracies. However, it is essential to understand that the fruits of our present actions alone shape our future destiny. We write our destiny. Let us understand how this happens.

When we perform karma, it is like tying a rope to our hand, the other end of which is tied to a parcel. This parcel represents the fruit of that karma. The rope that binds us to the fruit of our karma is called "Karmic Bondage." It is only when we receive the fruit of our karma that we are freed from the bondage of that karma.

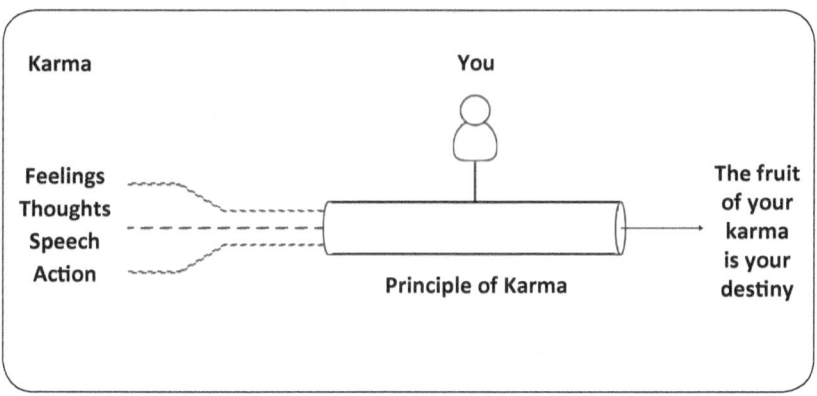

Nature is unbiased when it sends us our parcels. Nature decides when and who delivers the parcel. The parcels tied to us are our destiny. We keep receiving them from time to time, but the problem is that we often forget that we have ordered them ourselves through our karma.

For example, a student fails an exam despite performing well. Now, they and their parents may start blaming their destiny without knowing that they had created this parcel. They had plagiarized a friend's project the previous year without informing them and submitted it to the teacher in their name. And now they are suffering the consequences of this action. The student may not even remember their mistake and wonder why they failed the exam.

Similarly, when someone desperately needs help, but their loved ones do not support them, they may feel lonely and helpless. Just then, a stranger helps them in a manner they could not have imagined. They may perceive this as a divine miracle. But the reality is that this was their own parcel, a result of their good deed in the past, which nature returned to them at the right time.

Whether good or bad, nature gives back our parcels through different means. The medium could be anyone or anything: nature, some person, some incident, success, promotion, or sudden gain or loss.

Let us understand this with another example. Suppose you are going somewhere, and a passing car splashes mud on your clothes. Your clothes are soiled. What will you do then? First, calm down, align with the Source, and remember that this is your parcel from the past that the car driver delivered to you just like a delivery agent. Receive the parcel gracefully and thank him wholeheartedly for freeing you from an old karmic bondage. With this, you will bring back your tuning with the divine vibration.

Often people say, "This person, place, or thing is unlucky for me," or "My name is not compatible with my zodiac sign, so bad things happen to me. Had my name been different, it would not have happened." "My house has some energy defect and is not aligned with the principles of Feng Shui or Vastu Shastra. Hence, I am suffering from so many issues. Changing the house will resolve these issues." Remember that the delivery agent may be anyone or anything; everyone receives their own parcel. No power in the world can deliver someone else's parcel to you by mistake. So, whatever your name is, wherever you stay, whoever your companions are, your parcel will definitely reach you.

If we understand these principles of karma, we will certainly take responsibility for whatever good or bad happens to us. The day this happens, many of our negative thoughts will end. We will start focusing on resolving the problem rather than blaming others. This will bring back our tuning with the divine vibration.

In the next chapter, we will understand how to open our parcels while being attuned to the divine vibration so that they do not cause sorrow but joy.

Action plan:

1. Ask yourself - Am I prepared to take responsibility to remain in tune with the divine vibration?
2. Do you believe in the principle of karma and the justice of nature? Remember the incidents when you experienced the power of the principle of karma.

The First Step to Improve One's Tuning

When technology was not so advanced, people would listen to songs on the radio. A broadcasting center would transmit the signals of various programs which the radios in their homes would receive and play. The broadcasting center is a transmitter, and the radios are receivers.

Various radio stations broadcast their programs at different frequencies. We can turn the knob on our radio and tune in to those frequencies. Once the frequency matches that of the transmission by the radio station, we can listen to the programs transmitted by that radio station.

Similarly, there are many invisible transmitters present in nature that transmit programs in the form of mental vibrations. Some are positive vibrations, while others are negative. They are transmitted through different people. Among these, one vibration is transmitted directly from the Source. It is the divine vibration. We need to attune our body-mind mechanism, i.e., our body, mind, and intellect, to that divine vibration.

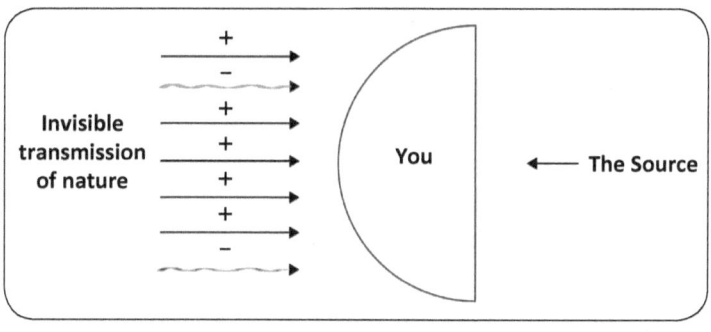

In the previous chapter, we understood the law of karma and the principle of karmic parcels. If we are able to implement it in our life and take responsibility for all the situations in our life, it means we have turned our radio's knob in the right direction. This will put an end to our mistuning and bring us in alignment with the Source. At this stage, we may not be fully aligned with the divine vibration and may experience some disturbance intermittently. To overcome this, we need to take the next step and fine-tune the knob again to align accurately with the divine vibration.

Now, all it takes is to take the first step

A couple was traveling with their children by train. After twelve hours, when they reached their destination, the children were as energetic as before, chirping with joy as they jumped and ran around. But the parents were exhausted. They appeared as if they had toiled hard while sitting idle on the train!

What could be the reason? The reason was not their age but their approach to life. As the train moved, the children also enjoyed swaying back and forth along with the train. When the train pushed forward, they also moved forward. When it pushed back, they moved back as well. There was no resistance, no opposition. On the other hand, what were the parents doing? They were continuously exerting themselves to sit firm without swaying with the train. When the train pushed forward, they would lean backward. When the train pushed back, they would move forward. Thus, they protested in every situation, making them tense during the journey and tired at the end.

Our life is also like the train journey, which rocks us forward and pulls us back from time to time. Those who accept every jolt in life as easily as the children, adjust and attune to it, and lead a smooth life. They always stay in tune. On the other hand, those who resist everything suffer from fatigue, anxiety, stress, and complaints and drudge through the entire journey of life.

The human mind tries to find its way in every situation and wants life to follow its whims. It always considers itself right and wants to see everything happen its way, using its own yardstick to decide what is right and wrong. It favors that which it likes and dislikes whatever does not match its liking. It regards various opinions and perspectives as wrong.

The mind wants everyone to behave according to its whims; everything should happen as per its wishes. In short, it wants every person and situation to toe its line. But does it ever happen? People begin to lose their alignment when things do not happen their way. This is the biggest reason for one's misalignment. They resist whatever is happening.

Resistance leads one to a complaining mode, and most complaints are unnecessary. For example, while waiting for a train, one may complain, "Why is the train late?" Even when the train arrives on time, they may still grumble, "Why did it not arrive on the same platform where I am standing?" If the train is on time and on the same platform, they may grumble, "Why did my compartment not stop before me? Why did it move ahead?" Their complaints continue even after boarding the train.

Many of us spend our entire lives complaining, "Why do some relatives behave differently? It hurts me." Our complaints continue even beyond our relationships. If it is raining, we complain, "Why is it raining now? I wanted to go out. It should have rained later." If it is not raining, we grumble, "There is so much shortage of water supply, and it is not raining yet." Or else, we think, "Why isn't it Sunday today? Why is it Monday? I am in no mood to go to work?" Or "Why is there no power? Why is the traffic light red?" We constantly resist something or the other and fall out of tune with the divine vibration.

If nothing else, we may keep complaining to God, "Why have You given me such neighbors? Why did You not bless me with a beautiful face? Why am I given such a weak body? Why am I given this relative?" In this way, our entire life becomes a bundle of complaints.

We can get rid of all these complaints in one shot by applying the principle of free flow. This principle entails us to stop resisting and start accepting every situation. Those who wholeheartedly accept everything, knowing it comes from nature, are attuned to the divine vibration. They accept all disturbances. If we find ourselves mistuned, we need to accept the situation. When we accept it, we take the responsibility of getting rid of all disturbances. When we stop resisting nature, we lead a harmonious life.

If we are unable to accept an incident in our present or from our past, which causes us pain when we remember it, we need to accept it with the understanding that it was our very own parcel that nature has delivered to us.

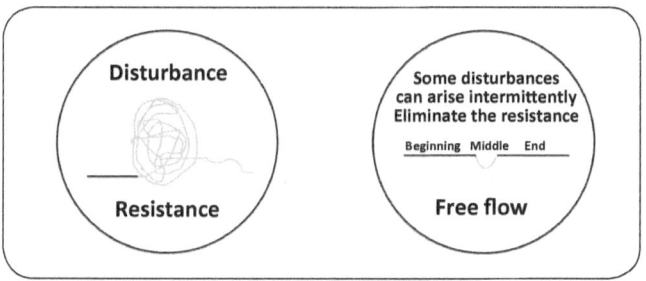

We need to accept it gracefully with gratitude and humility. Affirm to ourselves, "I accept this situation, incident, or shortcoming." As soon as we eliminate our resistance, we no longer experience sorrow.

Even if we are not entirely rid of the sorrow, it will indeed reduce to a great extent.

The more we eliminate resistance in life, the better-tuned and aligned we will become with the divine vibration of the Source. We will notice this through our own experience.

Agreement*

I, --------------------------(write your name here), on this date ----------in the presence of God (Divine vibration, Guru, nature) pledge that,

I am responsible for keeping myself aligned with the divine vibration of the Source.

If my mind resists any situation, I will ask myself, "Can I accept this situation and eliminate the resistance? Am I in tune with the divine vibration of the Source? Am I in love with it?" By doing this, I will be in tune again.

I am prepared to eliminate all complaints and remain aligned with the Source. If, for some reason, I become misaligned, then I take responsibility for correcting my tuning. No one else is responsible for it.

I will take the necessary steps to bring back my tuning.

Signature

---

*When we want to achieve something and we note it down in writing, the possibility of attaining it increases.

SECTION - 2
Aligning With the External World

Harmonious Tuning in Relationships

If one is experiencing deterioration in their relationships, an honest reflection will help them realize that resistance is often the cause of their sorrow. Parents are unhappy because their children do not follow what they say, while the children are unhappy because they think their parents do not listen to them. Husbands complain that their wives do not align with them, while wives feel their husbands always have their way. Bosses believe their subordinates do not follow their instructions, while the subordinates feel that their bosses are like dictators.

The point to be understood here is that nature has created everyone differently, not just in appearance but also in disposition. Everyone's thinking process, intellect, and experiences are unique. Then how can one follow and behave according to someone else's thought process? We need to look within and ask ourselves whether we act as per someone else's wishes. Would we like to be driven by others? The people around us are humans, not robots, who will behave as we program them.

Let go of the desire - "You be me"

As soon as one expects others to become like themselves and think and perceive like them, they have indeed turned their knob in the wrong direction and disturbed their alignment with the divine vibration.

Remember, people are not the same because God has made each one of us unique. This diversity is the beauty of the world. Consider each person as a musical instrument that produces different tunes. Someone plays like the flute, some like the drum, and some like the violin. If we want to align with them, we must maintain our own tuning first. Some are empty within, like a flute. They are extroverts. Some may be closed in like a drum. They are introverts. This is the beauty of nature. Just as all musical instruments are essential in their place despite being different, every human being is complete in themselves, even though they look different. No one needs to be like someone else. Everyone has their unique beauty.

If one instrument starts playing like the other, it will become mistuned. Hence, we do not try to create a flute tune from a drum. In the same way, we need to accept people as they are and remain in our alignment. The people around us, our relatives, play certain roles. We need to allow them to play their roles and stay firm in our alignment.

Accepting one another is essential, especially when two or more people live or work together in any setup, such as a family, office, or neighborhood. Otherwise, they will face conflict all the time. When two people with different tones have to sing together, a mature person will say, "You sing in your tone, and I will sing in mine." However, an immature person will keep insisting on the other person to align with their tone and spoil their own tune.

Therefore, we need to always ensure to be in tune first, no matter what, and not try to correct the tones of others. We need to tell ourselves, "This is how it is. The other person's tone is good as it is. I am not opposing it. I accept it." When we affirm this, we will attune to the Source, and our perspective will change. Then instead of finding faults in others, we will begin to notice their qualities and appreciate their uniqueness.

No-Resistance exercise

Whenever you feel resistance in relationships and become mistuned, you need to practice the following exercise to overcome this resistance.

Sit quietly with your eyes closed and focus on your breath. With each breath, start counting down from one hundred to one in your mind. Then, bring the person into your awareness about whom you complain the most or repeatedly think, "What you are doing is wrong. You are wrong, and I am right."

Tell him mentally, "You are right in your place, and I am right in mine. You are watching it from your side; I am watching it from mine. I am ending all the resistance between us."

Repeat these steps whenever you become angry about someone's behavior. You will observe an instant change. This will eliminate all resistance in your mind, increase your level of acceptance, and you will feel a different kind of freedom and happiness immediately. It is like a rope that was fastened to your hands is now let open. As you rid yourself of the resistance and your level of acceptance increases, your mind loses its stubbornness, negativity is eliminated, and you experience freedom.

Misalignment in the garb of love

If we reflect on the bitterness in our relationships, we will find that we become the most mistuned with the people we are more attached to, like our near and dear ones, spouse, parents, siblings, and children. It is still easier to eliminate resistance with outsiders, but it becomes a disturbance with our loved ones. We are often mistuned. The main reason behind this is our attachment to them, which causes their minor actions and reactions to affect us deeply. It disrupts our alignment with the divine vibration.

For example, a child did not eat his meal well. This trivial thing can make the mother upset and worried for the entire day. She may keep thinking all day, "He didn't eat well. How can he go on like this? Is he suffering from indigestion? I hope he hasn't eaten anything unhealthy outside. Should I cook something else for him? Or should I show him to the doctor?" and so on.

Nowadays, the most trivial things about our loved ones, especially our children, trouble us as if it is a huge calamity. This is because we do not regard them as separate individuals with unique personalities. Even if a grown-up does something independently or makes his own decisions, we feel left out and consider it a problem. We want to control their lives. If we eliminate this attachment, more than half of our worries will end. We will continue to remain in alignment.

To come out of this trap of attachment, first, we need to recognize this tendency. We need to understand that attachment is not love. It is a recipe for misalignment. Attachment binds us, whereas love sets us free. We need to repeatedly remind ourselves, "They are also the children of the same God who created me. The same God, who takes care of me, is also caring for them. I will fulfill all my obligations toward them. Whenever required, I will be available for any help or support. But I will never feel possessive or exert authority over them."

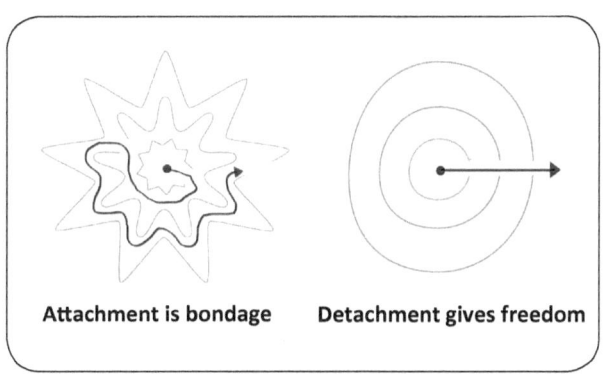

Attachment is bondage   Detachment gives freedom

Those who harbor love in their relationships and yet remain detached maintain mutual space in the relationships and enjoy healthy, everlasting, and sweet relationships. Such relationships are not a cause of burden or sorrow but rather the reason for love, happiness, and growth for one another. Therefore, we need to practice detachment and attain alignment with the divine vibration.

Action plan:

1. Every day, bring one person into your awareness for whom you feel resistance and practice the No-Resistance exercise.

2. Reflect, in which close relationships do you try to enforce your ways upon the other person? Is it due to attachment or non-acceptance?

3. One by one, bring all your near and dear ones into your awareness and say, "They are also the children of the same God who created me. The same God, who takes care of me, is also caring for them. I will fulfill all my obligations toward them. Whenever required, I will be available for any help or support. But I will never feel possessive or exert authority over them."

4. Note down the names of people for whom you feel resistance, fear, hatred, jealousy, or envy. Pray for their well-being from the bottom of your heart today. If it is difficult to write their names, note them down symbolically.

   1.
   2.
   3.
   4.
   5.

6

Release the Reins and Get Attuned

We often tightly hold onto the reins of control, believing everything will be fine if we are in charge, but this is not always the case. Let us understand this with an example.

Manu and Tanu were young neighbors and perfect friends. They would play together the whole day until they had a big argument. Their verbal fight grew into a brawl, leaving them badly hurt.

Hearing their screams, their mothers ran out to check on them. Being good friends, they tried to separate the children who were mangled in the scuffle and asked why they were fighting. Manu and Tanu each listed the other's mistakes in a way that made their mothers believe their child was right and the other at fault. As a result, both mothers began to quarrel with each other to support their own child. On hearing them, both fathers also got involved and started arguing with each other, causing a rift between both families.

Two days later, Tanu and Manu began laughing and playing like before. Their mothers were distraught to see their children playing together again, so they asked, "You had a fight in which he hurt you a lot. You had said that he is a bad boy who always troubles you. Then why are you playing with him again?"

Manu replied, "Did I say so? I don't remember. Tanu is my best friend; we always play well. Maybe I said that out of anger."

Tanu told his mother, "Our teacher says, 'Fight and forget. Don't take it to heart.' I missed Manu so much that I forgot about the fight. We both said sorry to each other. Let go of it, mummy. Whatever has happened is now the past. Now we are best friends again!"

Both clarified to their mothers and got back to playing again. The mothers kept wondering, "We fought with each other because of our children. The children have started playing together, yet we still hold grudges against each other."

As seen in the example with Tanu and Manu, children are always far closer to the Source. Therefore, although they lost their tuning for some time, they quickly regained it. But elders have stronger egos. They want to hold onto and control the reins of relationships. A little bit of conflict is enough for them to begin a fight. They bear grudges and endure them for years together. They take trivial things to heart and hold them for years. This mistunes them. To stay attuned to the divine vibration, we must become like children again by learning to let go of others' words and actions easily.

Regain the lost alignment with "Let go"

Water that flows is always pure and clear. But if it stops flowing and accumulates, it gradually becomes dirty, mossy, infested, and toxic. The same applies to the human mind. Our mind remains calm and pure when our stream of thoughts keeps flowing. However, when we hold onto certain thoughts and refuse to let them go, they can pollute the mind, making it toxic.

We need to consciously observe what we hold onto about others in our mind. What was said or done by others that we cannot let go of? Holding onto these grudges creates mental blocks, leading to psychological and physical ailments. Negative thoughts also result in undesirable parcels being received in the future.

To make our mind and intellect clear, healthy, and attuned to the Source, it is essential to seek forgiveness for our mistakes and then let go of and forget those issues.

When we sense a slight disturbance in our body-mind, we should immediately observe what kind of resistance has been created within us. What are we holding onto that is causing harm? We should accept it with the understanding that it is our own karmic parcel that we have received.

As soon as we let go of the negative words or actions of others, we experience a lightness within. We feel relieved from something that was stuck within. A burden is lifted, and we are free from stress. We are now attuned to the Source and can move forward with ease.

How to let go?

We need to seek forgiveness when we are at fault and forgive others when they are at fault. This way, we can regularly clear the garbage that accumulates in our mind. It is best to make it a part of our daily routine to perform this cleaning exercise before bedtime. Before retiring for the day, we can recall all the day's incidents. If we have hurt anyone through our thoughts, feelings, speech, or actions, we need to seek forgiveness from them mentally. Likewise, if someone has hurt us, we need to forgive them before going to sleep.

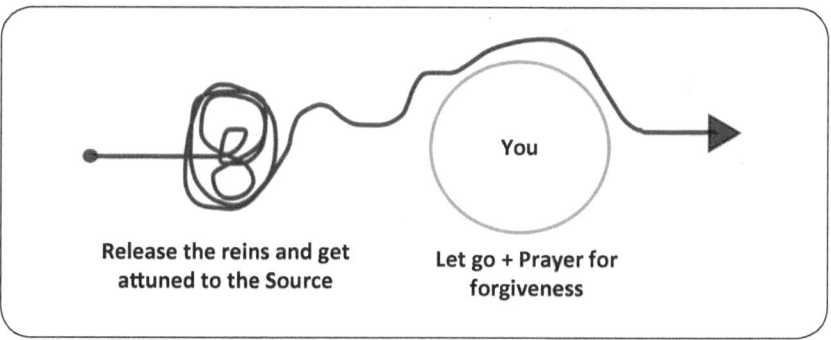

By forgiving others or seeking their forgiveness, we are not doing a favor to anyone. We purify our mind and attune ourselves to the divine vibration. Cleaning the kitchen before retiring for the day ensures we start the next day with a clean kitchen. Similarly, before going to bed, letting go of all the negativity allows us to wake up aligned with the Source instead of carrying forward the disturbance of the previous day.

It is better to seek forgiveness from someone in person if we feel comfortable doing so. We can say, "Please forgive me for hurting you through my feelings, thoughts, words, or actions. I will ensure not to repeat this." We can try to seek forgiveness in person, at least from our near and dear ones.

In some instances, we may not feel comfortable seeking forgiveness in person, or we may realize our mistakes later. In that case, we can recall that person in our mind's eye, seek forgiveness from them or forgive them mentally.

Consistently practicing forgiveness will bring wonders in our life. We will feel, "The very people who were bearing a grudge against me have now started behaving nicely with me. Relationships are improving. Problems are getting resolved. Everything is happening spontaneously in life. I am experiencing peace." We will feel connected to the Source.

Thus, we loosen our grip with the tools of "let go" and forgiveness. We can eliminate hatred, fill our heart with love, and spread love around us.

Action plan:

1. Recall someone with whom you are angry in your mind's eye. Accept your feelings for that person. Exercise "let go" with them and seek completeness.

2. Remember, "They are right in their place; I am right in mine." With this feeling, forgive them.

3. Mentally tell them, "I forgive you. You, too, please forgive me for hurting you. I will ensure not to repeat this."

4. Now release all your emotions about that person by saying, "Let go… let go… let go…"

5. Repeat this exercise with all those for whom you have felt negatively. Check your tuning after completing the exercise.

7

Attain Better Tuning with Completeness

Do you know what people regret the most on their deathbed? Regrets are not just about the negative words spoken or wrong actions performed, but also about not having said what they wanted to say, not having heard the words they wished to hear, not being able to complete some unfinished business or fulfill some of their unmet desires. Such incomplete things make them regret the most, and they die with a sense of incompleteness. Those who complete all their work on time, speak their heart out, and listen to everyone on time live in completeness. They never regret anything during their lifetime, at the time of death, or even after death.

Incompleteness disturbs the mind

What is the feeling of completeness? How does it work? Let us understand this with some examples.

If we give a half bar of chocolate to a child, they feel disheartened. But if we mold the same half so that although small, it appears complete, the child feels happy upon receiving it and does not complain. Why is this so? This is because the half bar of chocolate looks incomplete, but the small full bar looks complete. The child does not feel incomplete with the small but full chocolate bar.

A sick old man was admitted to a hospital, and all his relatives visited him except one. He was upset for not having met the absent relative rather than focusing on the other relatives who came to see him. That one missing relative created a feeling of incompleteness within him, which distressed him.

The feeling of incompleteness makes our thinking negative. We focus more on what we miss rather than what we have. Hence, it is best to stay away from this feeling, especially in relationships.

Completeness is essential in relationships

In life, successful relationships are those in which individuals can openly speak their hearts out without holding back anything. Such relationships are mutually fulfilling. On the other hand, when individuals hold back and do not communicate openly, relationships begin to fall apart. Each person creates their own version of the story, which can be far from the truth. This feeling of incompleteness slowly consumes them, hollowing them from within and causing them to fall out of sync.

When we do not express our innermost feelings, they linger within us. Sometimes, we go our entire lives without expressing them, which affects our alignment and leads to various psychological and physical ailments.

Sometimes, we may be comfortable sharing our feelings, but we refrain from doing so out of fear that it may worsen the situation. We may want to resolve these issues internally, and although we may succeed for a few days, these issues may eventually explode at the wrong time, further deteriorating the situation.

This can happen in any relationship, whether with family, professional associations, neighbors, or superiors. Therefore, we should speak our heart respectfully and appropriately, at the right time, and with humility. By doing so, we feel fulfilled and complete, which can help resolve issues and improve our relationships.

It is best to speak in such a way that the other person does not feel guilty while still being mindful of our own feelings and that of others. For instance, if we want to complain or disagree, we can say, "I understand your perspective, but I see things differently. This is how I feel. I may be wrong, but I wanted to share my opinion. I apologize if I have hurt you in any way." When we speak politely, in a non-complaining tone, the other person receives our message positively, leading to better results.

Imagine, there could be so many suppressed emotions within us, the recollection of which can disrupt our alignment with the Source. We may feel upset, regretful, or irritated. By expressing these emotions politely, we can feel free and empty within. This can also help quiet our mind's constant noise.

We should strive for completeness not only for the things we resist but also for the things we admire. If we appreciate something or someone, we should not hesitate to express our admiration. We should always express and appreciate all our near and dear ones and family members who care for us and play important roles in our lives.

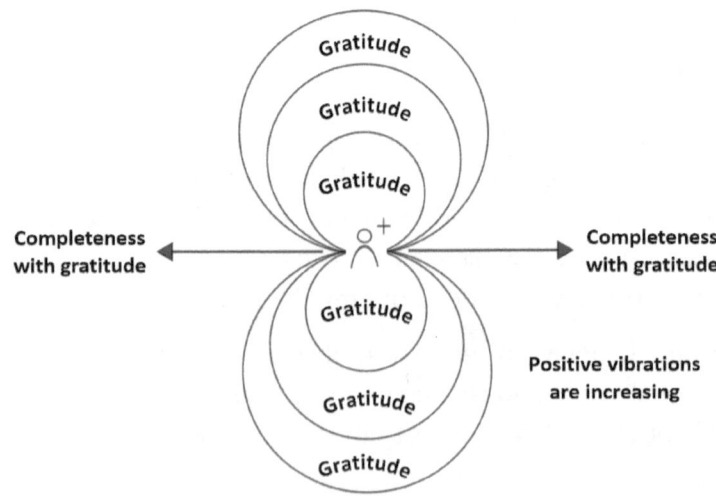

We receive help and support from many people throughout our lives, but we take them for granted. We fail to acknowledge their love, care, and service. We take our closest relationships casually and carelessly.

There are many people in our lives who allow us to live comfortably, but we never thank them for their support. For example, housekeepers, drivers, delivery agents, security guards, or anyone providing services. If they fall short of their expectations, we should politely give them our feedback and also appreciate them if they are doing their job well. This small step will make us feel much better and find ourselves attuned to the Source.

Incompleteness keeps trailing you

Have you ever noticed that when you leave some work incomplete, something unsaid, or any other incomplete feeling, it also appears in your dreams? If we want to say something to someone but cannot express it, we may end up doing so in our dream. The incompleteness trails us even in our dreams. We keep thinking about it even during sleep and watch related dreams. The incompleteness in our lives follows us throughout our lives and takes the form of injured memories that remain with us even in the afterlife.

Thus, if we keep accumulating puny sorrows and incidents without forgiving and letting go of them, they create a feeling of incompleteness within us, causing bondage in this life and even in the afterlife. Therefore, to the extent possible, we should seek completeness wherever we feel incomplete, lest our mind keeps gravitating toward the past. If we do not act on time, we cannot fully live in the present and leave this world with regrets and being mistuned to the Source.

Action plan:

1. Contemplate: What incomplete tasks do you remember and feel troubled about? List them and promise yourself that you will complete each of them one by one.

2. Do you dream about completing any incomplete task from your real life? Make sure to complete all such pending tasks.

3. Reflect on the relationships where you wanted to express something but didn't and are still bothered by it. Take steps to complete those conversations one by one.

4. Appreciate and thank those people in your neighborhood, office, or anywhere around you who provide services that you appreciate. Thank them for their efforts.

8

Alignment Changes with The Company You Keep

Once there lived a majestic and powerful king who became the father of twin sons. He had observed how same-aged brothers fought for the throne in neighboring kingdoms, resulting in catastrophic consequences for their families and the kingdoms. The king was inclined towards spirituality, so he decided to groom one of his sons to be a Self-realized saint and the other to be an emperor. But the predicament was about how both princes of the same family could fulfill such contrasting expectations.

As the princes were born at the same time and place, their horoscopes were the same. Hence, it was predicted that their fate would also be the same. When the king expressed his wishes to the queen, she reassured him, saying, "Don't worry. Please leave it to me. Your wish will surely be fulfilled."

When the princes were of school-going age, the queen sent them to two different institutions. One attended a spiritual school where sages and saints engaged in spiritual practices. He was taught how to detach from the illusory world and love God. Everyone in that school had only one purpose—to live in divine devotion and seek Self-realization.

The other prince went to the royal school, where he was trained in the highest knowledge of warfare, strategies, political science, and diplomacy. He was instilled with patriotic zeal and inspired to uphold the kingdom's welfare above everything else. His motto became "Live for the kingdom, die for the kingdom."

In due course of time, both the princes grew up. The one who attended the spiritual school became a detached, Self-realized saint, while the one taught in the royal school became a virtuous prince.

Although the royal astrologer predicted the same fate and destiny for the king's twin sons, the king was pleased to see that they had attained different positions due to their exposure to different environments.

Your company affects your alignment

The above story depicts how our company and environment greatly influence our personality and thought processes. As the saying goes, "A man is known by the company he keeps."

A dyer mixing different colors in different pots and dipping white cloth into each pot illustrates this point. Each piece of cloth gets colored in the hue of the pot it was dipped in. Therefore, our ancestors placed great emphasis on the company we keep, as it can make or break us. It has the power to improve or embitter us.

You may have observed that we feel good when we sit and have a pleasant conversation with someone. We feel comfortable in their company even if there is no conversation. Their mere presence makes us feel at peace. Conversely, some people make us feel low-spirited, and we may want to avoid them. We feel drained of energy if we talk to them for a while.

Each person radiates an aura influenced by the vibrations of their feelings, thoughts, and actions. As the person is, so is their aura.

When we come in contact with someone who radiates a negative aura, we feel negative vibrations. Conversely, we become more positive when we connect with someone with a positive aura.

When a tiny pebble is put in a vessel filled with water, it sinks and settles at the bottom of the vessel. But what will happen if the same pebble is dropped in a fast-flowing river? It will get carried away by the force of the water currents. Similarly, while one may withstand the attack of negative vibrations from a single person, a group of people with negative vibrations has a collective power to sweep him along with them.

Being in the company of drunkards can make it difficult to stay away from drinking alcohol. Eventually, one may succumb to the temptation and start drinking. Likewise, when the ignorant person, entangled in the illusory world, starts attending spiritual discourses consistently, they gradually begin to understand the true meaning of life and attune themselves to the divine vibration.

Achieve alignment with those with the divine vibration

To align oneself with the divine vibration, it is essential to understand what the divine vibration is. Being in the company of like-minded individuals may bring a sense of ease and relaxation, but it does not necessarily mean one is aligned with the divine vibration.

When we are amid people attuned to the divine vibration, we realize where we stand regarding our understanding and divine alignment. Therefore, it is beneficial to be in the company of people already on the path of listening to the truth of life, in service of this truth, and devotion. Their company will inspire us, and their experiences will address our doubts.

We may organize events in our surroundings and plan our daily routine to help us connect to the divine essence within us and awaken the thirst for divine alignment. Besides setting our daily routine to improve our tuning with the divine vibration, we should also allot time for regularly attending discourses on the truth of life, meditation, rendering service of the truth, reading, and contemplation.

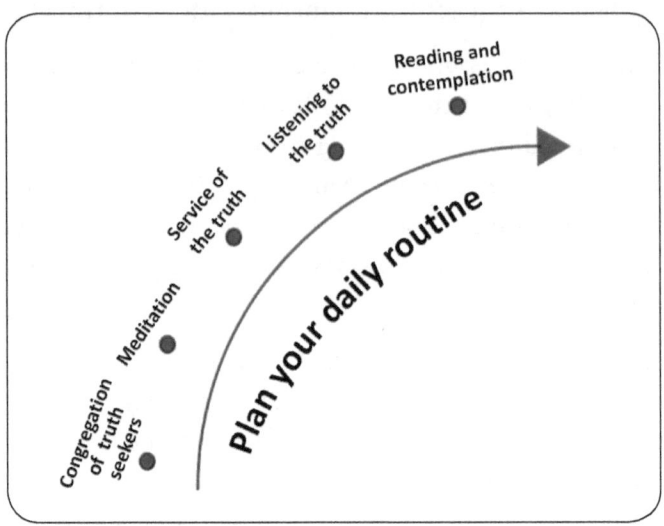

Attending spiritual discourses with other seekers helps to program our mind anew. New words and analogies we receive in such discourses can enhance our understanding of the deeper nuances of life. When people share their experiences of how they applied what they learned to overcome problems and became free from sorrow, a prayer for freedom arises, "If they can become free from sorrow, so can I." Such thoughts benefit us in our journey.

If we cannot find the right company, we can take the help of spiritual literature. We should not regard books as lifeless objects as they can raise our level of consciousness even more than a living person can. They can influence us as effectively as a spiritual teacher can. Sometimes a single line in a book can change one's life. Hence, we need to seek the company of the right books that give the right knowledge and understanding. We should read them with complete awareness and contemplate them. This will help to raise our level of consciousness and align with the divine vibration.

Thus, we need to be in the company of people with higher consciousness, and we will be automatically aligned with the Source.

Action plan:

1. Observe each person who comes in contact with you. Observe, in whose company your level of consciousness rises, you feel good, and in whose company you feel exactly the opposite. Observe what kind of people are more prevalent in your life.

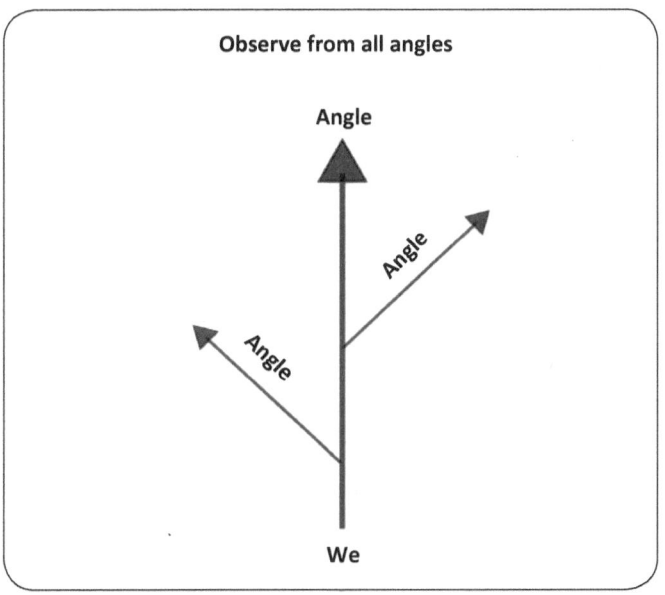

2. If you have any tendency or addiction, like smoking, drinking alcohol, excessive entertainment, excessive gossiping, resorting to lies, etc., contemplate, in whose company does it aggravate?

3. Observe how much time you spend in the spiritual company, such as attending and listening to spiritual discourses and spiritual sharing, contemplation, reading, meditation, etc. Try to increase the time you spend on these activities gradually.

Effect of Change on Alignment

The only unchanging law of this world is that everything constantly changes. What existed yesterday may not be there today. With time, many old things disappear, and new things come into existence. Today, the weather is not the same as before. Forests and animals are becoming extinct. With advanced technology, many new vehicles and facilities are available which were not there before.

If you carefully look around, you may exclaim, "This place has changed so much in the last few years!" If you meet someone after a long time, you wonder, "How much have they changed? I couldn't recognize them."

Our lives are in constant flux, both internally and externally. Change is an ongoing process. Sometimes we notice it, sometimes we don't. For example, have we ever realized that our body has changed entirely in the last few years? Over time, all the old cells in our body have died, and new cells have taken their place. This process of generating new cells and replacing old ones is continuous, and everyone undergoes it. This transformation happens so gradually and steadily that we do not notice it.

Changes that do not directly affect us or happen slowly often go unnoticed. However, when changes force us out of our comfort zone or require us to act differently, they can disrupt our alignment.

Being out of our comfort zone misaligns us

We start losing our alignment way before the actual change. When the effects of change are seen, we feel unsettled, perhaps even nervous, and think, "Oh! What will happen to me now? How will I cope? What challenges will I have to confront, and will I be able to manage it all? Everything was smooth and settled; now I will have to start all over again." Even before the change has happened, our radio starts creating disturbance; our mind starts chattering.

This happens because when we remain in the same situation for a little longer, we get into a comfort zone. A comfort zone is a convenient space where we know everything. We know what to do, when, and how to do it. Our body and mind have got habituated to being in that state.

For example, a homemaker starts her daily routine when she wakes up. She knows what to do when and the preferences of each family member. Everything is at the tip of her fingers. These activities do not bother her. However, if she were to carry out the same activities in someone else's house, she would not be able to perform them with the same ease and efficiency. She would feel stressed and require more energy to complete them. This is her comfort zone. Our home, office, and the places where we live our daily lives become our comfort zone.

This happens because the details of every daily activity and how we perform them get registered in our subconscious mind. Then based on this programming, our subconscious mind operates automatically, like a machine. Due to this, we do not need to think or understand much while performing activities within our comfort zone, and everything happens automatically.

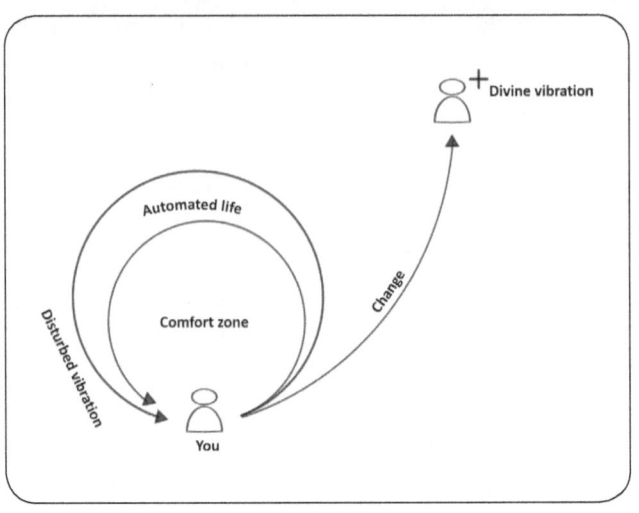

Consider a person who wakes up in the morning with their mind flooded with thoughts about an upcoming presentation scheduled in the afternoon. Although their mind is preoccupied with the presentation details, they get ready, have breakfast, and drive to work. Although they are unaware of all these activities, everything happens on autopilot.

But imagine if they had to make this presentation at their client's office, where they have never been to before; would everything happen with the same ease? No, it would not. They would become more conscious of the time and their attire. They would keep an eye on the route and the traffic signals. Obviously, they would spend more energy presenting it to a new client at an unfamiliar place and feel more stressed.

If a slight change in their routine makes them so conscious and alert, imagine how they would cope with a significant change! They would be subject to much more stress and doubts. They would need to leave their comfort zone to deal with this change.

Everyone likes to be in their comfort zone. However, when life brings in the next change, most of us get upset; we feel a resistance within, which disturbs our alignment with the divine vibration.

Accept the novelty and avoid the mind's chatter

Often, elderly people reminisce and remark, "Back in my days, it was different…" They often glorify their past experiences and criticize current events. This is possibly due to their reluctance to embrace change, as they may resist it actively. Even if they seem to be enjoying the benefits of modern times, they may still mentally reject them.

Whenever someone rejects a change, it disrupts their alignment. For example, in the winter, they might say, "Oh, how cold it is! Summer was better." And in summer, they might say, "Oh! It's so hot! I'm sweating. If only winter came early." They do not accept winter in the winter, and summer in the summer, despite knowing that this cycle of seasons has been ongoing for ages and will continue. People disturb their tuning by resisting trivial inevitable things.

Many years ago, when the computer was invented, many people resisted it. They wondered what humans would do if computers replaced human effort; how would they earn and survive? Some people's livelihoods were affected by this technological shift, but it was only a temporary phase. Those who adapted to the new information technology wave stopped working in old ways and adopted new ways. As a result, they were able to acquire better jobs than before.

Today, we all can witness the transformation that computers and advancements in information technology have brought about. More employment opportunities have been created worldwide, and work gets done more efficiently, faster, and better. It has touched every sphere of activity and brought progress in almost every field. It has changed the lives of people and resources. However, initially, people regarded this change as a calamity.

Imagine a person who has always had a fixed routine every day. They wake up at the same time, eat the same breakfast, take the same route to work, etc. However, one day, they are forced to break their routine and take a different route to work due to unforeseen circumstances.

Initially, they feel anxious and uncomfortable because they are used to doing things a certain way. But as they continue taking this new route, they notice new things, such as a beautiful park or a quaint coffee shop. They also begin to appreciate the change in their routine and the excitement of exploring new things. Eventually, they realize that their old routine was limiting their experiences and that change can be good.

This story also teaches us the importance of accepting and embracing change, even if it may initially feel uncomfortable. Sometimes, the things we fear or resist the most can lead to new opportunities and growth.

Change has not stopped; it will continue perpetually. If we resist it, it will continue to bring about a mix of joy and sorrow, disrupting our alignment. But if we accept change as a routine process, we will look at it with awe and appreciation, eagerly waiting for new scenes to unfold.

If aligned with the Source, we will become instrumental in bringing about novelties and innovations in the world. This is because nature brings about better changes in the world through those tuned and receptive to the Source.

Consider the recent pandemic, which shook the whole world. It was a massive change for everyone. Initially, most people lost their attunement. But later, even those who never cared for their health and well-being understood the importance of a healthy lifestyle and robust immunity. They worked towards improving their immunity and started focusing on good health.

People have started becoming more conscious of their health since the pandemic. They have taken a break from their busy schedules, let go of their stressful lifestyle, and begun spending more quality time with their families. They have given up drinking harmful beverages and focused on eating and drinking healthily. They have become careful with their diet.

Moreover, the medical field has seen rapid development in its research. Achieving faster and better research in such a short time is unprecedented. With time, we will find that in our attempt to safeguard ourselves from the pandemic, we have saved ourselves from many other diseases and started leading better and healthier life.

Keep reminding yourself that change is inevitable

We started to realize the benefits of the pandemic after it was over. But how can we realize it and retain our tuning even when a situation is ongoing?

Just as a guitar's strings must be neither too tight nor very loose for optimal playing, we can remain aligned with the divine vibration only when we are neither attached to the present nor resistant to change.

When we find ourselves stuck in our comfort zone, we need to remind ourselves, "Change is the law of life. Everything is changing. Whatever my situation today, it will surely change tomorrow."

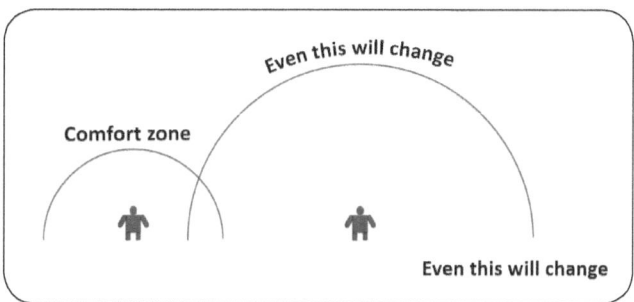

If we are unhappy with our current situation, we will feel relieved knowing it is not forever. If the current circumstances have become our comfort zone, we need to break free from them and accept them.

We need to confidently tell ourselves, "Even this will change one day, and something new will emerge, for which I am open and ready. I accept and approve of the change that is to come. God is with me, so I have nothing against any change. I can adapt to change, easily let go of the old, and embrace the new."

As soon as we adopt this attitude, our resistance will dissolve, and we will find ourselves tuned to the divine vibration.

Agreement

I, ---------------------------(write your name here), on this date ----------in the presence of God (Divine vibration, Guru, nature) pledge that,

I fully accept changes in any aspect of my life, whether it be my livelihood, environment, place, or routine activity.

If I cannot accept a change, I will try my best to find the reason behind it, whether I have lost any good opportunity, my growth is hindered, or it has affected my health adversely.

I say with complete confidence, "Whatever the change is, I accept and approve of it completely. God is with me, so I don't fear any change."

Now, I have become more flexible than ever before and am prepared to move forward with time.

Signature

SECTION - 3

Aligning With Your Inner World

10

Autosuggestions for Attunement

On the outskirts of a village stood a giant peepal tree that the locals believed was haunted. According to their belief, if someone passed by the tree at night, ghosts would possess them, making them sick for a few days.

One day, a monk and his disciple visited the village and decided to stay under the haunted tree for the night. The villagers tried to dissuade them, but they remained firm in their decision. When the villagers still insisted, the monk reassured them, "Don't worry! I know of a secret mantra; chanting it will keep the ghosts away. So, go home rest assured and let us also sleep peacefully."

The villagers came to check on the monk and his disciple the next morning, anticipating unusual symptoms and behavior due to the influence of the ghosts. To their surprise, both were perfectly normal and happy. The villagers were amazed to see them unaffected by the ghosts.

A farmer approached the monk and requested, "It would be a great favor if you could share the mantra with me. This peepal tree is situated on what was my farm earlier. I was unable to work peacefully because I was afraid of ghosts. My farm has become barren now, and I have no way to make a living."

The monk told the farmer, "My son, there are no ghosts on the tree. It is an illusion of your mind, a mere superstition. Go ahead and plow your farm without any fear. Nothing will happen."

But the farmer was skeptical. He insisted, "No! That tree is haunted. I have experienced it myself. One night, I came here to check on the crops and saw some weird shadows flickering around the tree's trunk. I heard some whispers too. I was scared, and the next day, I fell sick."

The monk realized that the farmer's belief in ghosts was due to his superstition and fear. The farmer mistook the shadow of the swaying branches of the peepal tree and the sounds of the animals and beetles as ghostly activities. He had fallen sick due to his fears. But he did not explain this to the farmer. He thought for a while and said, "Alright! I will tell you the mantra. But it will work only if you have unquestioning faith in its power; else it will be futile." The monk whispered the mantra into the farmer's ears, "You are a bodiless ghost. I am a bodily ghost. We both are ghosts; we both are like brothers. The one who has troubled me will be punished."

Although the farmer found the mantra strange, he believed the monk's words. He kept chanting the mantra intermittently while visiting his farm at night, and to his surprise, he felt perfectly fine the next morning. The so-called ghosts on the peepal tree did not affect him.

The next day, the farmer went to thank the monk. The monk blessed him and left the village with a smile. On the way, the disciple asked the monk, "Sir, that was a strange mantra; how did it work?" The monk explained, "The mantra didn't work. It was the farmer's faith that worked. By chanting the mantra, the farmer was convinced that he was safe and nothing would happen to him. Earlier, when he fell ill, that was also the effect of his negative belief, 'There is a ghost. It will possess me, and my health will surely deteriorate.' Our beliefs affect our mind and body the most."

Direct your thoughts toward faith

This story highlights a profound message: Our beliefs, whether positive or negative, manifest when we hold them in full faith. Research has shown that the placebo effect can be a significant factor in medical treatments. Some studies indicate that placebos can be as effective as actual medication in some instances since it is faith that drives the treatment.

It is essential to have faith in the right things to stay in tune with the divine vibration. Clinging to negative beliefs can quickly throw us out of alignment. Always remaining aligned with the divine vibration is an art that can be mastered with practice. For this, we must identify stray thoughts and turn them in the right direction.

Often people go astray and lead their life carelessly in a stupor. To counteract this, taking intermittent breaks and reflecting with full awareness is crucial. For instance, practicing Pranayama (breathing exercises) helps us breathe consciously, which benefits us immensely. Similarly, thoughts are constantly running. We need to understand the laws of thoughts, be mindful of them daily, and direct our thoughts accordingly. *

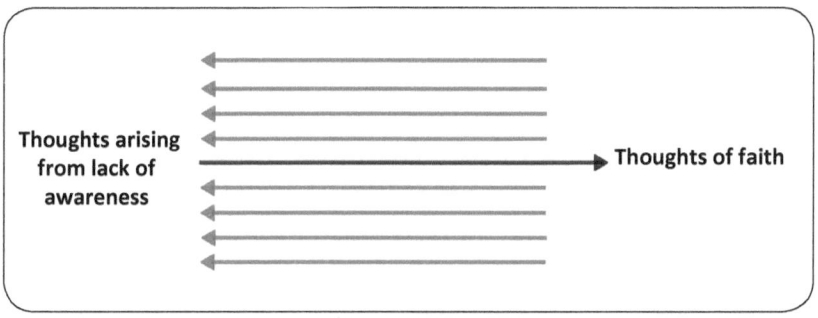

---

* To understand more about the dimension and laws of thoughts, read the book "The Source …Power of Happy Thoughts" by Sirshree.

Direct your thoughts with autosuggestions

Since childhood, we have been taught to perform physical actions, but no one has taught us how to think. Consequently, our thoughts run astray and most often tend to be negative. To change this, we must learn to create affirmative statements and keep repeating them mentally. This will help change our vibrations and eliminate our fears, weaknesses, shortcomings, and tendencies. It will also empower our body, mind, and intellect with the power of faith, boost our inner strength, and attune us to the divine vibration.

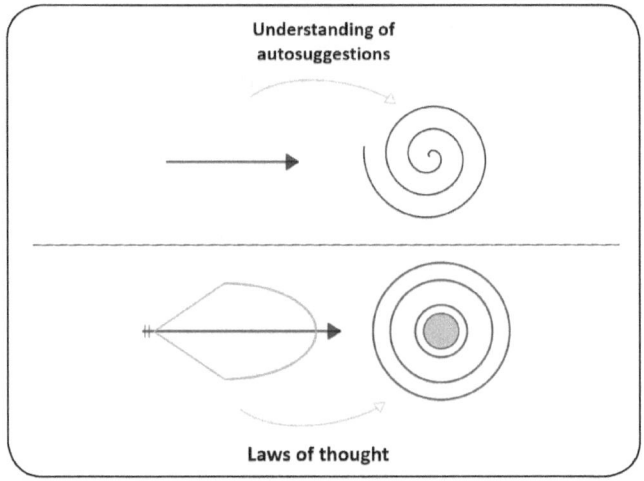

Each person's challenges are unique, so each of us can benefit from diverse autosuggestions. We need to experiment with different autosuggestions and find the ones that resonate most with us and help us to attune to the divine vibration.

Here are some examples of autosuggestions. Considering our shortcomings, we can also form such statements and keep repeating them with full faith.

- If we are scared of some occult or supernatural power like ghosts, we need to say, "I am God's property; no evil can touch me."

- If we are scared of falling sick, we need to say, "I am God's property; no illness can harm me. I am healthy and will always remain healthy. Health is my birthright."

- If we have problems in our relationships or estranged relationships, then we need to say, "I am in favor of love, joy, and peace. I forgive everyone; everyone forgives me too. I love everyone; everyone loves me too."

- If we fear that we cannot complete any work on time and in the right way, we can say, "I am complete; hence all my work gets happily completed on time and in the right manner."

- If we fear facing problems, we can say, "The problem that does not kill me makes me stronger."

- If we are anxious about our future, we need to say, "I believe in the divine plan of life. One who cares for even the tiny creatures under the sea also cares for me."

Benefits of autosuggestions

If we keep repeating such autosuggestions, our vibrations will begin to change. Soon, we will notice changes in our life. This evidence will strengthen our positive beliefs, allowing us to overcome our shortcomings, weaknesses, and fears and emerge as a strong person. By doing so, we will attain all the best gifts that nature offers us, which were once stalled due to our negative thoughts.

The process of giving autosuggestions and reaping its benefits can be likened to that of a farmer sowing seeds in the soil. A farmer selects the best seeds to ensure a bountiful harvest. After sowing the seeds, he neither leaves his farm unattended nor does he repeatedly dig out the soil to check whether the seeds have germinated. He only takes care of it with complete faith. He sows the seeds at the right time. He waters his crops daily, treats the soil with fertilizers, protects his fields from animals, and remains surrendered in faith. He stays calm until the yield is ready.

We also have to do the same. We need to sow the seeds of autosuggestions in the soil of our mind. By repeating them again and again, we empower and reinforce them. We should not intermittently check whether they are showing any result, "Has something happened? Has something changed?" We need to nourish the seeds with assurance, provide them with the sunshine of love, the fertilizer of joy, and remain steadfast in our faith until it yields its fruit. Remember, we do not consume the seeds; we only sow them in the soil to reap the benefits of the fruit they produce.

The way the farmer protects his crops from animals and birds, we too must protect our thought seeds from any negative influences during the waiting period. We must remain vigilant, avoiding negative influences that could falter our faith and disrupt our alignment. During this testing period, we must ensure that our alignment remains intact with unwavering faith.

Only when the farmer sows the seeds does nature begin to work on them in the unseen. Similarly, when we keep repeating autosuggestions, nature begins to act on those thought seeds. However, it takes time for us to see the results. During this waiting period, our virtues like faith in divine providence, devotion, patience, and conviction help us.

We only need to change our inherent thoughts and emotions and then watch everything happening with love, joy, and peace. Sometimes, the mind may say, "I can't do this task. It seems difficult." In such instances, we must immediately replace that thought with the help of autosuggestion, "Yes, it is difficult if I do it alone, but God is with me, and everything is possible with God." By doing so, we get immediately attuned to the divine vibration. This way, we must learn this unique skill that can transform our life.

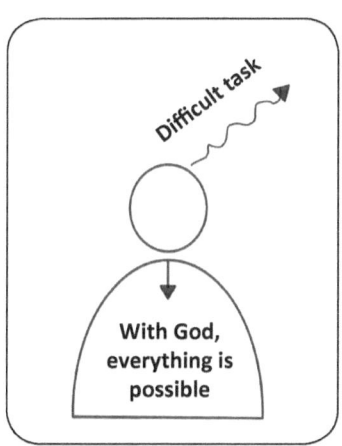

Action plan:

1. Reflect on any negative thoughts or beliefs like fear, disappointment, insecurity, inferiority complex, worries, etc., that disrupt your alignment with the divine vibration.

2. Note down all the reasons why you think negatively and how they affect your physical and mental health.

3. Write down powerful autosuggestion statements for each negative thought and belief, and keep repeating them in your mind. You may refer to some of the autosuggestions in this chapter or create your own.

4. For example, suppose you keep thinking, "No matter how hard I work, I don't earn enough. There is always a scarcity." You can use the autosuggestion: "Nature has an abundance of everything for everyone, including me. I am receiving everything in abundance. I only need to change my perspective and thoughts."

5. Whenever negative thoughts arise, repeat your chosen autosuggestions and feel the change in your vibration.

Effect of Feelings on Our Alignment

Many individuals are mindful of their actions and work to maintain their alignment with the divine vibration. They also try to choose their words carefully, thus avoiding harm to themselves and others that could disrupt their alignment.

They may gain significant control over their thoughts through meditation and other techniques. However, they may still feel that something is missing, as their alignment can still be lost despite their efforts. In this chapter, we will explore some possible reasons for this.

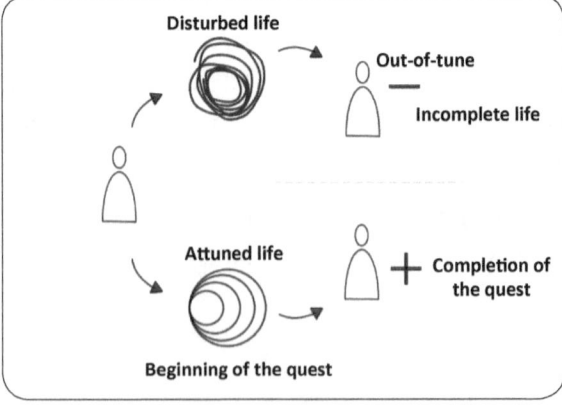

One who seeks finds

There is a saying, "You see what you want to see." But how does this work? Let us understand this with an example.

In an exhibition, there was a painting with an upright flute and the Sudarshan Chakra (a disk with spikes, the potent weapon of Lord Vishnu in Hindu philosophy) spinning on top of it. The visitors were asked, "What did you notice first in the painting – the flute or the Sudarshan Chakra?" Some noticed the flute first, while others noticed the chakra.

Despite viewing the same painting, why did different people notice different things? The reason is that people tend to see what they are predisposed or inclined to see, not what is in front of them.

Extending this saying further, "We tend to see things the way we are." Our thoughts, beliefs, and desires shape our perception of the world.

When you look at this painting, what do you notice first? Introspect and think. It is not about being right or wrong but understanding yourself and enhancing your understanding.

In the Hindu ethos, the flute symbolizes devotion, and the chakra represents power or material attraction. Those who see the flute first may have a natural inclination towards devotion and gentleness, whereas those who perceive the chakra first may lean towards power or force.

To further illustrate this point, let us examine another scenario. A girl wanted to buy a yellow dress but could not find one. Now wherever she went, be it the market, college, or neighborhood, she noticed many girls dressed in exactly the same yellow she wanted. This was the first time this had happened. She thought, "Nowadays, everyone seems to be wearing the yellow I like!" It was because she had never previously paid attention to anyone's yellow dress, but now she did not miss noticing a single one.

You may have also experienced that once you have decided to buy a specific car model, you suddenly start noticing that car more often because you are constantly thinking about it.

This phenomenon is known as Frequency bias or Frequency illusion.

In reality, everything surrounds us - the good and the bad, the positive and the negative. What we see or don't see depends on how we are. A virtuous individual will perceive goodness in others, while someone with many flaws and negative thinking will perceive shortcomings and negativity in others. Their thoughts and feelings are in sync with their reality. No matter how much they attempt to, they cannot think or feel positively about anyone.

Let us extend the saying further, "People see what they want to see. They desire to see what they are and discover what they truly seek."

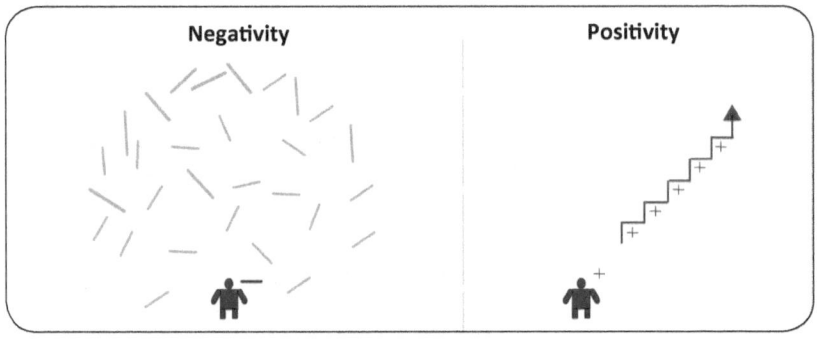

Initially, many may have differing views on this idea. They may say, "We sincerely wanted some things in life but didn't get them. Although we tried hard, we did not receive them."

This may have happened to many people who did not get what they wished. What could be the reason? Before we get into its detail, let us read about an incident related to Swami Vivekananda during his student life.

In his early years, he was known as Narendra. Being very intelligent and inquisitive, he would always think logically. He had many questions related to God: Does God exist? Can we perceive God? Has anyone ever seen God?

Whenever religious preachers would visit his city, he would meet them and directly question them, "Have you seen God?" They would be taken aback as nobody had ever asked them such a direct question. Many preachers and prophets of different religions visited the city of Kolkata, but none could answer him in the affirmative. Despite that, he continued to meet them and repeatedly asked the same question.

After some time, in his quest for Truth, he got associated with a spiritual organization named Brahmo Samaj and became its member. This organization was involved in service to the masses. Hence, Narendra was satisfied after joining this organization, but he did not feel fully satisfied until he achieved what he was seeking. Every time new religious preachers would visit the Brahmo Samaj, he would ask them the same question, "Have you seen God?" In response to his question, they would either become dumbfounded or ramble. Narendra was disappointed and thought, "There must be at least one person on this earth who would have seen God."

During one of such religious gatherings, he met Sri Ramakrishna Paramahansa, the priest at the Goddess Kali temple. Narendra had heard a lot about him and asked him the same question, "Have you seen God?" Sri Ramakrishna Paramahansa promptly replied, "Yes, indeed! Just as I see you, so have I seen God in the same manner and also talked to God! If you also wish to see God, you can do so." Finally, Narendra met the Guru, who could say with conviction that he had seen God.

After that, under the guidance and company of Sri Ramakrishna Paramahansa, Narendra attained the state of divine alignment wherein he could experience God-consciousness.

This story teaches two important lessons. Firstly, Swami Vivekananda achieved what he desired despite facing many challenges. He met a guru who put all his doubts and queries to rest, ultimately making him worthy of Self-realization.

Secondly, he also met a lot of devotees, religious preachers, and prophets who would discuss God intellectually but could not proclaim that God can be perceived. This was because they revered God and claimed God's omnipresence in all living and non-living beings, yet they still believed that God could not be perceived. As a result, they did not have an ardent quest to realize God and contained themselves with what they had received.

Sri Ramakrishna Paramahansa was perfectly aligned with the divine vibration, always immersed in God. His every feeling, thought, word, and action was guided by the Source. Hence, he could assert with unwavering conviction, "Yes, we can see God."

As our feelings, so our faith

There is a similar story from the childhood of the Indian Saint Namdev. His family worshipped Lord Vithal and would offer food to His sacred idol daily. One day, while Namdev's father was away, his mother asked him to offer food to God. Namdev did as he was asked to and, with great joy, returned the empty plate to his mother. She was surprised because she knew that the idol could not have eaten the food; offering food to God was merely a symbolic ritual. However, Namdev had seen God eating the food and was perplexed why his mother could not believe him.

Namdev never perceived God as an idol but as a living entity, so he believed God had eaten the food he had offered. He always perceived Lord Vithal as a living divine being. However, his mother referred to Lord Vithal as an idol and did not see the living essence in Him. She wondered how the idol could eat the offering. Unlike Namdev, she was not aligned with the divine vibration and was not awakened.

To summarize, whatever we feel strongly about, whatever we invest our feelings in, so will be our faith. This, in turn, influences what we see in the world, what we seek out, and ultimately achieve.

Merely aspiring for something, thinking about it, and acting on it is not enough to achieve the desired results. We must have intense passion in alignment with our goals. To be aligned with the divine vibration, our feelings, thoughts, words, actions, and even writing must be aligned in the same direction. Then we can attain whatever we desire: happiness, prosperity, contentment, peace, health, joy, or anything else.

When our feelings, thoughts, words, and actions are aligned in the same direction, we can accomplish great things. However, when they are not aligned, our alignment with the divine vibration gets disrupted, and we experience inner turmoil, confusion, and a lack of direction. Let us explore this in detail in the next chapter.

Action plan:

1. Contemplate how convinced you are about the presence of the divine vibration. Has this conviction emerged from your feelings or some hearsay?
2. When do you feel the need to get aligned with the Source? Is it always present, or only when you experience sorrow?
3. Contemplate how you feel when you are aligned with the divine vibration. Are your feelings and actions aligned in the same direction or scattered?

Mind Your Emotions, Master Your Life

Our emotions hold the greatest power in our lives, guiding us in every step. As our emotions, so are the thoughts that arise within us. As our thoughts, so is our speech. Our thoughts and speech are reflected in our actions. As our actions, so is our life; they determine our present and future. Thus, emotions are at the very core of our lives. So, we need to pay utmost attention to our emotions and care for them. Unfortunately, this is not often the case.

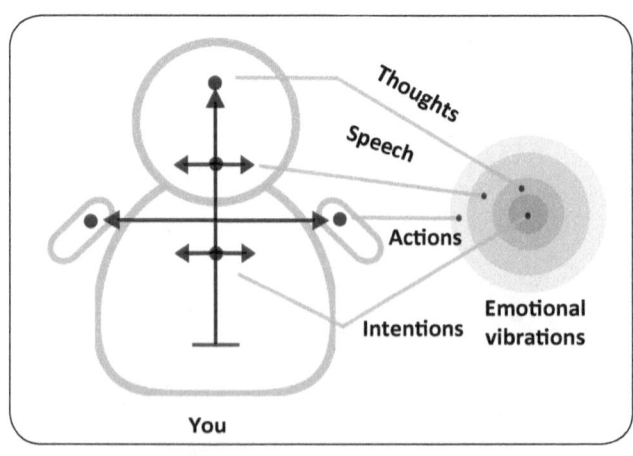

Many of us forcibly restrain ourselves from taking action or speaking out due to fear of negative consequences. However, our mind continues to chatter within. With increased awareness and understanding, we begin to become mindful of our emotions and thoughts and progress on our inner journey. We focus on keeping positive thoughts and avoiding negative thoughts.

Despite our best efforts, we do not always remain in alignment with the divine vibration and may often find ourselves out of tune. We may not achieve what we desire in life, and even if we do, we may not experience the happiness and contentment we were seeking because our emotions are not aligned with our accomplishments. When it is time to celebrate our achievements, we may be caught up in an emotional rut due to other challenges. As a result, we often experience some turmoil in our lives.

Disadvantages of contradictory prayers

When we desire something but intend something else, i.e., our desires and intentions are not in sync, then we are doing contradictory prayers. This means we pray to nature for something to happen, but our emotions negate that prayer. Consequently, we remain out of tune, regardless of whether our prayers are answered or not. Let us understand this with an example.

A family was based out of Pune. They had their only son. The mother wanted her son to seek admission to the best engineering college in the country, just like her neighbor's son. So, she enrolled him in the best coaching institute in the city and ensured that he followed a healthy diet, sound studies, and a disciplined routine. However, as the exams approached, she started having concerns such as, "O God! Next year he will move out to the hostel. He has always stayed at home so far. I don't know how he will stay alone in the hostel. It would be better if he gets admission into a college in Pune. But what if he gets admission to a college in Delhi? It is so cold there; he can't bear the cold weather and will immediately fall sick. Will he be able to come home for the Diwali festival? All the festivals will go unobserved without him. We will feel so lonely without him. It would have been better if he studied in Pune itself." Unfortunately, her thought process also influenced her son.

The son could not secure admission to his desired college and enrolled in an engineering college in Pune. Despite studying hard, attending the best coaching institute, and doing his best in the exam, his mother was upset that he could not get into the country's best college.

What can we attribute this to? Though the mother wanted her son to seek admission to the best college, her emotions contradicted her prayers. She wanted her son to stay with her in Pune, and when her emotions were fulfilled, she was still unhappy because her mind wanted something else.

We often face such conflicts where our desires are not aligned with our emotions, thoughts, speech, and actions, resulting in failure to achieve the desired outcome.

Consider another example of an employee who aspired for promotion at his workplace. His boss informed him that his promotion was being considered by the management, and he would most likely get it. However, the employee's mind got clouded with confused emotions and thoughts: "If I get promoted, I will have to leave this office and move to another city. I will miss my friends and colleagues. I will have to search for a new house and school for my kids in the new city. The cost of living in the new city is quite high. What if I don't like the job or my new boss? I am comfortable with my current life and don't want any changes." With these conflicting thoughts, the employee unknowingly blocked his upcoming promotion.

We should avoid making such mistakes. Our emotions and doubts should not prevent us from receiving good things in life. To maintain our alignment, we must comprehend and align our emotions with the divine vibration.

We should always live with the assurance that "God always provides us the best and will continue to do so. No matter where and how we are, God will always care for us." By surrendering ourselves to God, we must leave all the "ifs and buts" to Him. This is the only approach to silence the unnecessary chatter of the mind.

Before we offer any prayer or wish for something, we must observe whether our emotions, thoughts, speech, and actions are aligned or scattered. First, ensure they are brought into alignment. When in alignment, any work we do will make us feel complete and contented throughout the day.

The reason for being out-of-tune is within us

Many people blame the world for their misalignment without realizing that their world comprises their activities and the people surrounding them. They see the world as the cause of sorrow and distress. Consequently, they isolate themselves and turn to the path of God. They become monks, visit temples and mosques, attend spiritual discourses, perform prayers, worship God, and so on. When asked why they attend discourses or visit temples, they say, "Nothing is left in the world. We want to worship God and stay in His refuge."

But do they really feel that way? Do all seekers attain the same results by listening to the same discourse and performing the same spiritual practices? The answer is "No," as everyone's emotions and experiences differ.

People often claim that they attend spiritual discourses to attain the Truth, but their true motivation may be to seek relief from their sorrows and troubles. Even if they experience temporary relief from these burdens in the company of the truth seekers, their emotions may eventually pull them back into worldly pursuits. This is because they never truly desired to detach from the world and pursue the path of Truth in the first place. Instead, they were compelled to attend spiritual discourses as a means of escape from their sorrows and troubles. Once free from these sorrows and troubles, they do not feel the urge to attend spiritual discourses and quickly return to their old ways of life.

True devotees like Saint Meera, Saint Kabir, and Swami Vivekananda, who earnestly quest to attain the Truth, alone attain Self-realization. This is because their emotions, thoughts, speech, and actions are aligned and attuned to the divine vibration. Those who could maintain their alignment could sing divine hymns and dance in divine bliss while leading a worldly life.

We cannot escape from the world because we are a part of it. Instead of trying to escape the world in the guise of renunciation, we need to work within ourselves while we fulfill our worldly roles. We should be alert and safeguard ourselves from falling out of tune. We need to bring alignment in our emotions, thoughts, speech, and actions. This means feeling what we think, expressing the same in our speech, and putting it into action. By doing so, we need not have to escape anywhere.

Action plan:

1. Contemplate, when did you experience not achieving the desired results despite putting in the best efforts?

2. What were your feelings while working towards the desired goal? Were you indulging in contradictory prayers?

3. Check your emotions when you fall out of tune with the divine vibration. Check whether your emotions, thoughts, speech, and actions are aligned. For example, you may want to achieve a certain goal but also want to avoid the hard work involved in achieving it or after it.

Ask Pivotal Questions to Get Aligned

An entrepreneur was struggling with a lack of customers for his business. He tried different marketing strategies, but nothing seemed to work. One day, he attended a networking event, and someone asked him, "What makes your business unique?" This question shook him up and made him realize that he had not been highlighting his unique selling proposition effectively. He started thinking about ways to showcase his unique value proposition, and soon he started seeing an increase in customers. That one question asked at the right time helped him get back on track and put him on the path to success.

It is essential to ask the right question, at the right time, in the right manner. However, it can be challenging. It is the first thing that needs to be done to overcome any problem.

One pivotal question can shake us up, awaken us, take us off the wrong path, and guide us on the right path. The right question asked at the right time can bring back our alignment. It can give our thinking a new direction. It will not only help us solve our problems but also help us remain fully attuned to the divine vibration.

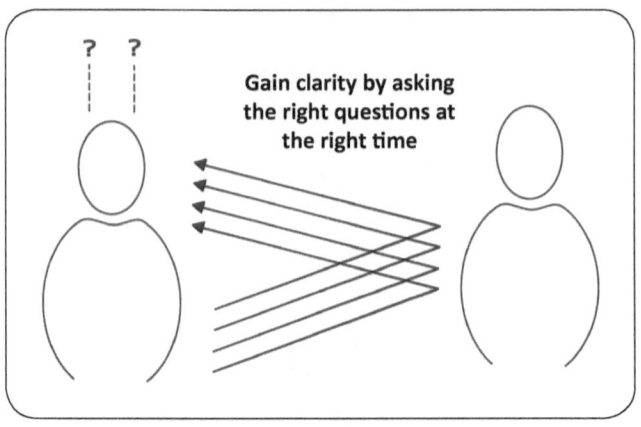

In this chapter, we will understand the power of such pivotal questions.

Raising a pivotal question – the first step toward awakening

After falling out of alignment with the divine vibration, those who asked the right question at the right time could regain their alignment. Additionally, they became forever free from the possibility of being caught up in the antiques of the ego, tendencies, and ignorance. Let us understand this with the help of some examples.

Saint Dnyaneshwar was an enlightened medieval saint from Maharashtra in India whose spiritual awakening and literary work have kindled devotional fervor among the masses for many generations. Before him, his father had renounced the world in his spiritual pursuit but returned to worldly ways by marrying and nurturing a family.

His return to worldly ways was regarded as blasphemy by the orthodox priests of those times. He and his family were banished by the committee of priests and ostracized from society. As penance deemed by the committee, he and his wife had to give up their lives by undergoing a water burial.

Saint Dnyaneshwar and his three siblings were very young at that time. The punishment and humiliation inflicted upon their family by society kindled a burning question within Saint Dnyaneshwar, "Why was my family subjected to such brutal punishment? Was it justified? Was it righteous?"

His thirst for knowledge was so intense that he received answers from his elder brother, Nivruttinath, who explained that the sole reason for such treatment was ignorance in society. This ignorance was due to the non-availability of knowledge in their native language, as the spiritual scriptures were confined to the privileged class, who presented them to the innocent and ignorant in a distorted form to safeguard their vested interests.

This question gave a new direction to Saint Dnyaneshwar's life. He took up the mission of dispelling ignorance in society. He rendered the Bhagavad Gita in the native Marathi language, stirring society towards a mass awakening through a devotional revolution.

Similarly, when Siddhartha Gautama encountered sufferings around him, questions arose within him, "What is the root cause of suffering in the world? Is there a final solution to it?" These questions tormented him so much that he relinquished his royal life and embarked on the journey to seek the answers. Finally, he did find the answers and spread the wisdom that dispels sorrow from life. People continue to benefit from this wisdom even today.

When the little child Nachiketa asked his father, "To which God will you offer me?" his father answered in a fit of rage, "To death! I will donate you to Lord Yama, the Lord of death." This made Nachiketa wonder, "What is death? How does it happen? Why does it happen? What happens after death?"

The story goes that he approached Yama, the Lord of death, and asked him these questions. Lord Yama urged him, "Ask for some other blessings—longevity, progeny, wealth, rulership of a planet of your choice, celestial dancers of your choice. But don't ask me these questions." Nachiketa replied, "All material things are transient and would not confer immortality. I want nothing else but the final answers to my questions." Finally, Lord Yama had to reveal the secret of life, death, and a state of liberation beyond it. Later Nachiketa documented this knowledge in the Vedic scripture called "Kathopanishad."

In the previous chapter, we read about Swami Vivekananda's pivotal question, "Can we see God?" This one question paved the path to Enlightenment for him.

As a child, Saint Meera innocently asked her mother, "Who is my husband?" Her mother pointed at Lord Krishna's idol and said jokingly, "He is your husband." Meera embraced this answer so deeply that she upheld Lord Krishna as the only God in her life. This question stirred an intense, innocent devotion within her, paving the way for her Enlightenment.

This highlights the power of questions. But the question must illuminate the way like a lamp amid the darkness of all the negativity, dilemmas, and confusion. Such questions are priceless and arise only by divine grace. They enable us to make the highest choices and attune us to the divine vibration, leading us to liberation.

What is your right question?

Let's understand how an engineer could save himself and his family in challenging times by asking the right question.

During the recent pandemic, his company put him on "leave without pay" for four months as part of their cost-cutting measures. However, the engineer's household expenses remained the same. Unfortunately, he could not find another suitable job based on his professional skills.

So, he had to find some way to run his household in those four months. He took up a temporary job as a courier delivery agent, which would go on under any circumstances. This job was far below his qualifications. He was often confused and frustrated with his work.

Whenever he lost his alignment, he asked himself, "Why am I doing this job?" As soon as he would receive the answer from within, "For taking care of my family and for their happiness," he would calm down and continue working happily. After getting attuned to the divine vibration, he would thank God, "During such difficult times, when so many people are jobless and unable to meet the necessities of their families, God has at least made this job available to me, with which I can run my family and take care of them."

"Why am I doing this job?" Asking this right question at the right time helped him easily sail through the difficult four months while his fellow engineers remained idle at home, cursing their expensive lifestyle, destiny, and challenges. He managed to resume work after four months without any stress.

While this question may seem ordinary, it was precious and pivotal for that engineer. Asking this question helped him tide through financial doldrums and remain attuned.

Like him, everyone faces challenges where they lose their alignment with nature. At such times, people usually become nervous and lose their courage, finding themselves helpless and not knowing how to overcome the situation. They lose their alignment completely. However, the first step is to get out of the negative feelings by asking oneself the right pivotal question.

Just as the engineer regained his alignment by asking himself the right question, we, too, must find our right question and ask ourselves that question repeatedly. As soon as we do this, we regain our lost alignment. In situations where we curse others, we begin to thank them. Being able to express gratitude in the worst cases is a sign of regaining complete attunement.

Some all-purpose pivotal questions

We all face different situations, our understanding varies, and different questions arise within us that guide us toward the right path. Nevertheless, some all-purpose questions that can be commonly used are given below. They will help elevate our consciousness, contemplate the right direction, and regain our attunement to the divine vibration.

Q. 1: Am I aligned with the divine vibration at this moment?

We will gain awareness when we ask ourselves this question. We will check our state. If we are out of tune and experience any disturbance of the mind, we will eliminate it and get attuned to the divine vibration.

Q. 2: Who am I?

This is the most powerful question in the universe, which enables us to discover our true Self. It is the fundamental question that can lead to Self-realization. Whenever we assume ourselves as a separate individual, get entangled in the illusory world, and are trapped in the whims and fancies of the mind, we can remind ourselves of our true nature by asking this pivotal question. All the resistance within will automatically cease, and we will find ourselves aligned with the divine vibration.

Q. 3: Is Thy (God's) will mine?

We can ask this question when things are not happening as we would like. We need to understand that everything is happening by God's will. If our wish is not aligned with God's will, we are not aligned with the divine vibration. We need to accept everything as God's will, "Let Thy (God's) will be mine," to regain our alignment. This pivotal question helps us let go of our desires and align with the divine will.

Q. 4: Can I forgive others and myself?

Whenever we hold grudges or negative thoughts for ourselves or others, we need to ask ourselves this question immediately. We will overcome the feelings of anger, hatred, and guilt and regain our alignment. Since forgiveness is a divine virtue, it is also present within us. We need to seek forgiveness from others and also forgive others for all the mistakes committed knowingly and unknowingly.

Forgiveness is a powerful and effective quality that calms us just as we pour cold water to extinguish a blazing fire. The more forgiving we are, the better aligned we are with nature.

In this way, we need to inculcate the habit of asking pivotal questions and remaining aligned with our true Self.

Action plan:

1. Contemplate any pivotal question that arose within you that changed the course of your life and attuned you to the divine vibration. Ask yourself that question again. Observe whether that question still holds good today or has already been answered.

2. If you feel confused or doubtful in the present situation, ask yourself the right question and guide your life in a new direction.

3. Why do you want to remain aligned with the divine vibration? If your alignment is disturbed, what will be your first step? Contemplate this question, note down the answer you receive from within, and place it where it is easily visible as a constant reminder.

14

The Story that Disrupts Your Alignment

Two close friends spent most of their time together. One loved telling stories. He would narrate fictional stories with deep feelings, vivid expressions, and flow that breathed life into them. Even those listening to them would lose themselves in the story and feel as if they were its part. His friend knew about his skill, would listen to the stories delightfully, and admire his talent.

This friend was fond of listening to music. He would always carry a small radio and listen to soft music. He was so adept at listening that he could listen to his friend's stories while also paying attention to music. But things began to change over time.

The storyteller friend was so skilled that his friend would get emotionally charged and stuck in the story's characters. Gradually, his focus shifted from music to stories. He started believing that the stories were his friend's real-life experiences. He felt a deep connection with the joys and sorrows, the highs and lows, the pleasures and pains in the stories. He was so engrossed in his friend's tales that he even stopped sensing the soft music from the radio, unaware that the radio had run out of battery and stopped playing songs. He would laugh and weep with his friend's stories, feeling as if the joys and sorrows were his own.

You may wonder whose story this is. This is our very own story! The friend narrating the story represents our body-mind mechanism which comprises our body, mind, and intellect. The other friend who listens to the music represents our Consciousness, our true Self, the Source, the real "I." Some people get so engrossed in their bodies that they start assuming themselves as their body. Consciousness drives the body like a vehicle and is distinct from the body. We are the Consciousness, the Self.

The slow, melodious music from the radio that brings us joy symbolizes the divine music within us. To live life the right way, we should always listen to the divine music within, stay attuned to it and listen to our own and others' stories without getting attached to them.

That means we should listen to the stories but avoid getting entangled in them, believing them to be true. As long as we don't get entangled in the make-believe stories, we stay in tune with the divine vibration. But as soon as we get attached, our alignment gets disturbed, and we start hearing chaotic noise instead of divine music.

What is our story?

Every person's life is a story that begins when they are born. They are not the only character in that story; there are many characters around them. Every character has a name and role, such as parents, siblings, friends, relatives, colleagues, etc. But if you ask them, "Please introduce yourself," will they tell you the truth that "I am the divine Consciousness that dwells in this body?" No! They will start telling you about their character's script, "My name is so-and-so, I live in this city… These are my parents. I work at this organization, and my designation is this," and so on. They will narrate the story so passionately that despite knowing it is imaginary, you will forget about it and believe it to be true.

The world is like a huge stage where different bodies play their respective roles. God has written a very versatile script for the world. Every character enacts their role according to their story. All individual stories are part of a magnum opus script. Some characters get added or removed from the individual's story. People spend their whole life considering this drama to be the reality. It becomes their truth.

However, everyone's story ends only when they realize their true Self. Then they detach themselves from the story and see everything from a bird's eye view, being the Self. They realize that the Self alone is the author, the actor, the producer, and the director of this entire script. The Self alone plays different characters through the medium of all bodies.

After understanding and experiencing this, they do not get entangled in any story, neither in their own body nor in anyone else's. They only focus on the divine music emanating from their heart and stay aligned with it. Such an attuned and harmonious person lives life in free flow. They do not get affected or involved in any story or get trapped in the web of attachment, hatred, pleasure, or sorrow because all these dualities thrive only when they are attached to the story.

A seasoned professional actor does not get personally affected by whatever happens to the character they portray on screen. They play their role, even a tragic one, with joy. Similarly, the one attuned to the divine vibration plays their worldly role with the joy of realizing their actual existence without being attached to anything.

How to complete an incomplete story – Story witnessing meditation

Before you begin this meditation, read and understand the steps below. Then sit with your eyes closed in the posture of your choice.

1. Recall your life story from childhood until now. Watch the story with the new insight you have gained. This life story that

you believed to be yours is not your own but of your body. Watch it with detachment as if you are sitting far away and watching its movie on the screen.

2. You may recall many moments in the story that could pull you into the story and arouse intense emotions. You may feel happy or sad, dissatisfied or regretful. Some scenes may have happened as you wished, while others may have worked against your wishes. Scenes that did not turn out as you wanted may have caused you more pain. In this way, while watching the story, wherever you feel stuck, ask yourself these questions:

   - Who do I believe I am while watching this story now?
   - Whose story is this - mine or my body's?
   - Who am I? The consciousness that is knowing the story, or this body? If I am the Consciousness, then this story is complete because Consciousness is complete in itself. Nothing can be added to it or reduced from it.
   - Am I in tune with the divine vibration now, or am I feeling mistuned due to some emotion?

3. Feel the divine vibration of aliveness, the conscious existence within, while watching the story. When you watch the story, being attuned to the divine vibration with detachment, you experience freedom. You perform all your activities in a free flow with the intuitive mind, free of all bondages and chattering of the mind.

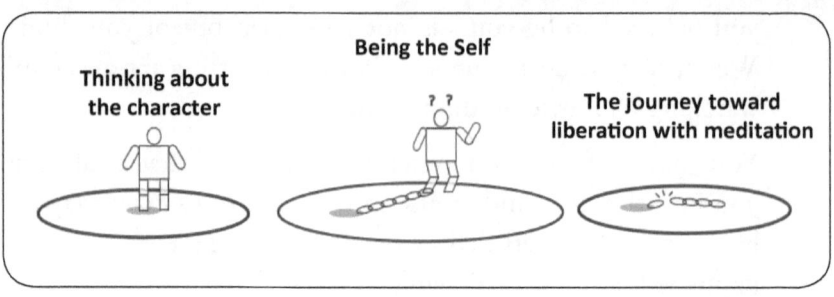

Action plan:

1. Contemplate which stories you get more involved in, due to which you forget to remain in tune with the divine vibration.

2. Practice the story-witnessing meditation daily for a few days and observe whether you feel neutral to your life story.

3. Contemplate how long you remember, "My presence is distinct from my body," and when do you forget it?

15

The Alignment of the Body, Mind, and Intellect

A senior officer bought a new swanky car for commuting to the office and hired a skilled driver with years of experience. He installed all the necessary accessories in the car and filled fuel to capacity. He explained the entire route to the driver.

On the first day, they left for work with great enthusiasm. However, after a while, the driver stopped the car on the side of the road, saying, "Sir, the vehicle appears to be having some trouble. It seems that the tuning of its parts may be causing some issues. I'm finding it difficult to control the car as it's responding with a delay; it takes about two seconds to stop when I brake. Additionally, shifting the gears causes the engine to shut down, and there are alignment problems with the steering wheel. I'm concerned that if we continue driving, we risk an accident. To resolve these issues, I suggest we have the car tuned before driving."

The officer was disheartened and thought, "I'm unable to enjoy the comfort of commuting to work in luxury despite buying such an expensive car, hiring a skilled driver, and ensuring that all aspects of the vehicle, including the paperwork, fuel, and accessories are taken care of."

Despite all the preparations, the car did not work properly due to a glitch in the instrumentation. In this example, the car represents our physical body. It is futile to have control over our mind, intellect, and feelings and align them with the divine vibration if our body is not in control, just like an unbridled horse.

Our body is the tool that transforms our thoughts, feelings, and intentions into action. However, if this tool is like a car that has broken down, our life journey cannot be successful. We cannot complete our work properly on time or achieve our goals. When we want to meditate, it will resist, "No, I want to watch TV now." When we want to go for a morning walk, it will push back, "I need to sleep a little more." It will continue to create hindrances. Hence, along with our mind, intellect, and emotions, our body must be properly tuned, which needs training.

The body is a medium, not a showpiece

The body is a medium of expression, but we have turned it into a showpiece. The body should be healthy and follow our instructions. It should fully support us in attuning to the divine vibration. A disciplined and obedient body is fit for this purpose. When the Source tells us, "Wake up, leave the bed," the mind, intellect, and body must adhere to it. When the Source tells us to exercise or meditate, the body and mind must cooperate. If the body signals, "Don't eat more than this," we should resist the temptation to indulge our sensory cravings and stop eating.

Nowadays, people have become more conscious of their physical fitness. They take care of their health and diet. However, it is essential to be clear about why we should care for our body. The body is indeed important, but it is important as a medium to fulfill our life's purpose and express divine qualities, not as a showpiece to be flaunted. But today, this understanding is being lost.

If given two options, what kind of body would you choose?

1. A healthy body that does all your work but does not live up to the popular standards of physical beauty.
2. An unhealthy body that does not perform all your work properly but looks attractive. It may even help you win a beauty or macho contest.

Nowadays, people desire to have the second type of body. Many women compromise on their diet and exercise for a so-called zero figure. They aim to become slim rather than healthy. Similarly, men focus on building their muscles rather than being fit and healthy. And for this, they get lured by advertisements and consume costly supplements. The focus is entirely on how their bodies are perceived, whether they are considered beautiful. In this way, their bodies become the cause of their downfall. Let alone tuning with the Source; their bodies cannot even accomplish basic goals properly.

Therefore, first and foremost, we must change how we perceive our bodies. We must consider the body a medium of expression, not a showpiece. We must instill it with discipline, good health, and flexibility so that it supports us. We must improve its health with proper diet, exercise, and lifestyle. Let us understand an exercise to enhance the flexibility and efficiency of our body.

Adding a little extra to the ongoing effort

In this exercise, we will align our body with our intentions. Our body should respond in alignment with our intellect. When our mind and body align with and act upon what our intellect thoughtfully decides, the three are in harmony. Such a body can become the medium for attuning to the divine vibration.

Suppose you want to do an activity for twenty minutes. For instance, you may want to walk on the treadmill, meditate, exercise, study, contemplate, brainstorm, or engage in some form of service for twenty minutes. You can add twenty seconds extra to these twenty minutes.

Adding a little extra effort, we communicate to nature that we are prepared for even more constructive activities. Our body will break its limits and support us in doing this. We can perform such small experiments to make our body disciplined and flexible.

Preparing to see the body as a medium

Most people are so attached to their bodies that they assume they are their bodies. If there is any ailment or disorder in the body or its parts, they take it as if it is happening to them. They cannot separate themselves from their bodies. As a result, the pleasures and pains of the body dominate them. They focus on giving comfort, rest, and pleasure to their body.

To overcome this attachment, we must change our perspective and remind ourselves, "I am not this body. I am using this body as my vehicle. I am its operator and controller."

Now, we will practice meditation to help us detach from our body. First, read the instructions and understand them before closing your eyes.

- Close your eyes and sit erect but relaxed.
- Relax your mind and focus on your body. Feel the outline and shape of your body.
- You don't have to visualize your body. Just focus on the parts of the body that you can sense. It could be a triangle, square, pentagon, or hexagon. It could be with a singular outline or fragmented into parts. Sense your body as it is right now, not as you have learned to think about it.
- Now feel the sensations on your body. Some parts may feel painful, while others may feel light or heavy. Some parts may feel dry or damp due to sweat, heat, or cold. Just feel it without judgment or resistance.

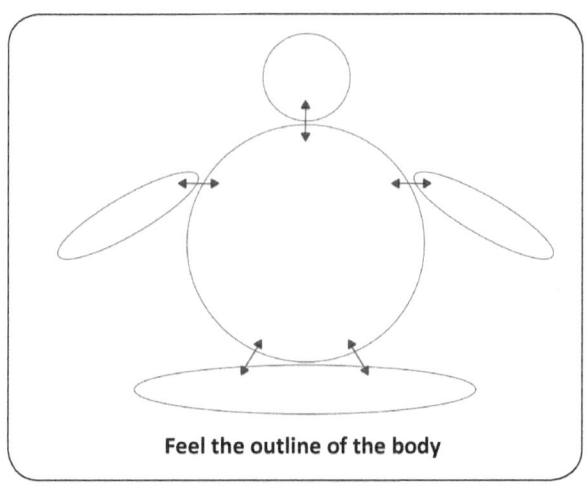
Feel the outline of the body

- When you sense the body this way, you perceive it from a distance and realize that you exist apart from it. You are the knower of the body. Now tell yourself, "Whose shape is this? This is my body's shape, not mine."
- Tell yourself, "I am not this body. I am the one who is feeling the shape of this body." In this way, feel your body from a distance, with detachment.
- Tell your body, "You are my companion. I love you. Always support me in my spiritual practice. Help me attune to the divine vibration. You can do this. You have the strength; you are ready. You are my well-wisher. Thank you very much for this support. Thank you, thank you!"

With this meditation, you can change the tuning of your body and make it positive and supportive so that it will align with you in achieving your goal.

You can study the life of any saint or self-realized soul. Their body never overpowered them. Their body would always obey them. They respected their body, but they were not slaves to its whims. They never got entangled in their body. We should also strive so that our body becomes a medium to attain divine alignment.

Agreement

I, ---------------------------(write your name here), on this date ----------in the presence of God (Divine vibration, Guru, nature) pledge that,

I will prepare my body to fully support me in all healthy activities like meditation, exercises, hard work, walking, studies, or rendering service.

I will not treat my body as a showpiece or a means of enjoyment but as my friend, perceiving it positively as a medium to help me perform the right deeds.

I will perform the exercise of "adding a little extra to the ongoing effort" daily and understand which habits of my body break or change with this exercise.

Being firmly convinced that "I am not this body," I will reinforce this understanding by regularly practicing the meditation explained in this chapter.

Signature

SECTION - 4
Aligning With Your True Nature

16

God Also Seeks Mutual Alignment

To be happy and content at all times, we need to stay in harmony with the divine music, be aligned with the divine vibration, and flow freely in life.

Just reflect, is it only man's desire to always remain aligned with God? Is this attunement just a human necessity? Is it a one-sided relationship? No. It is a two-sided relationship. The love between a devotee and God is mutual. God also wants to be in alignment with man – His supreme creation – so that He can express Himself at the highest level through human life.

For example, when a great musician performs, their fans come from far and wide to listen to them. It is not just the audience that needs to listen to good music; the musician equally seeks an audience to listen, understand, and appreciate their musical expression. This attunement between the musician and the audience is a mutual need and desire.

Just as a great musician needs listeners to appreciate and showcase their musical expression, God, too, desires to express and appreciate Himself through people who are attuned to the divine vibration.

When individuals are in alignment with God, they become a channel for His highest creations in the world. However, when people fall out of tune, God sends hints through various channels to guide them back to alignment. It is up to each person to be receptive to these hints and correct their tuning. This attunement between humans and God is a mutual need and desire, and it is through this alignment that God can fully express and appreciate Himself.

How does God guide us?

A boy was unsure and confused about which field to choose for an excellent professional career. He began praying to God, "O God! Please guide me to resolve my confusion." One day, while he was traveling by bus, the passenger sitting next to him got off the bus, leaving a booklet behind. Curious, the boy picked up the booklet and started flipping through it. To his surprise, he discovered that it contained detailed information about career possibilities in a particular field, including institutes for admission, entrance examinations, and the required preparation. As he read through the booklet, he realized that he had always been interested in this field but lacked the necessary clarity to pursue it. Grateful for this unexpected guidance, he thanked God for the help and support.

Those who have faith in God seek His guidance through their prayers, and God guides them in some way or the other. It can also be said that God first raises His call from within those He wants to guide through their prayers. They pray and surrender all their worries to God and feel empty. Then, they become receptive to God's guidance. When such people receive God's hints, they understand them quickly. However, those who lack receptivity do not understand His hints.

The boy got upset and asked God for help after all his efforts were in vain. Until then, he was out of tune. But it was good that when God gave him the thought of praying, he complied and prayed. Hence, God could help him.

Therefore, first, we need to increase our receptivity to seek God's guidance. Let go of the ego that makes us feel "I know everything" and ask God for guidance. Express our worries through our prayers to Him. Have complete faith in Him and trust Him. As soon as He listens to our prayers, He begins preparing to make the required guidance available to us.

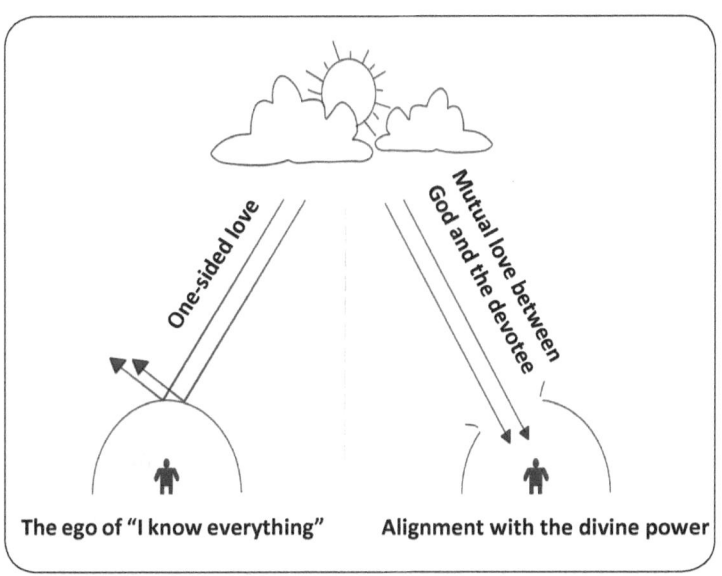

God can guide us through different channels such as a book, friend, billboard, or newspaper that convey information to help us find a solution to our problems. We may also come across something written somewhere, or a powerful thought may suddenly arise within us, providing an entirely new direction. Sometimes such divine thoughts occur within us. If we are alert and receptive at that time, we can grasp those hints; otherwise, we cannot.

Thus, there is no need to lose patience or become disappointed when we face any problem or confusion because doing so will misalign us with the divine vibration. We cannot grasp the hints sent by God then. We need to remain aligned and happy and pray to God in full faith. Through our prayers, we must convey to God that we need

His guidance and be aware and receptive to grasp His hints. People who are highly aware can receive God's hints faster.

How to seek God's guidance?

You may wonder how God knows we have full faith in Him and are aligned with Him. He realizes it from our smile and happiness. This is our feedback to God. Just like little toddlers walk with their parents, holding their hand, carefree and confident, in complete joy, because they know that their parents are with them, who love them, and care for them. They feel entirely safe with their parents. We, too, must feel the same in God's presence.

If we are sad and worried, we may inadvertently convey to God that we do not trust Him. Therefore, it is first essential to assure God that we trust Him with our smile and happiness. A happy person is like a magnet that attracts happiness, positivity, and the right guidance, while an unhappy person draws problems, confusion, stress, and negativity. Therefore, the first ability we need to instill in ourselves is to be happy in every situation and pray to God happily.

When this happens, understand that God has also started working immediately from the other side. He has started looking for the suitable medium through which the required help and guidance can reach us. But what if God does not find such a medium? How will the guidance get to us?

God can work in mysterious ways and may use the channel of the people around us to provide us with insights, advice, or solutions to our problems. However, many people have a habit of constantly getting into arguments, blame game, and conflicts with those around them. They often miss out on the guidance that God may be trying to send them through these very people.

If we are constantly engaged in negative interactions, we may not be open to receiving divine guidance. Instead, we may remain stuck in our argumentative ways and miss out on the opportunities God provides us to learn, grow, and align with the divine vibration.

Therefore, we need to reflect on our behaviors and relationships and strive to cultivate a more peaceful and harmonious environment. This can not only improve our relationships with others but also open us up to the divine guidance that God may be sending our way. Those who have cordial and harmonious relationships with their neighbors, relatives, and colleagues receive much information through them. God's guidance may likely be hidden in that information.

For instance, a person wanted to inquire about the best law colleges in Mumbai for his son's further studies, but he constantly fought with his neighbors over trivial matters. Now, he had a neighbor whose cousin was a professor at the best law college in Mumbai. He could have received the best guidance for his son if only he had a cordial relationship with this neighbor.

The moral of the story is to maintain good relationships with everyone, be happy, and speak politely because we never know through which medium God will help and guide us.

If we are praying happily and keeping all the channels around us open through which God can guide us, then we only need to patiently wait for God's guidance with wonder and appreciation and be aware to recognize it when we receive it. This is not difficult; our inner voice will tell us, "This is exactly what I wanted. This is surely God's guidance."

If we align our lives with the divine vibration and live by God's guidance, our lives will be filled with love, joy, and peace. God's purpose will be fulfilled because His guidance is the best, and nothing else in the world can give us that.

Action plan:

1. Reflect on the occasions in your life when you have received unexpected help from some unseen source and exclaimed, "This is nothing short of a miracle!" Did you recognize that God arranged that help for you? Did you thank Him for that?

2. When your work progresses miraculously or you receive some help in life, do you consider the source of that help to be God or the medium through which you received the help?

3. Contemplate how many channels are available in your life through which God can provide you help or guidance. Have you shut down any of these channels? If you have, try reopening them.

4. Contemplate how much you help God. How often do you become a channel for God to help or guide others?

17

Be in the Feeling of Havingness

We may often experience situations where everything seems perfect, yet we fail to achieve the expected outcome. Many say, "Everything I do starts well and progresses well too, but just before its completion, something goes wrong, and some challenges arise. All my hard work, money, time, everything goes in vain. Don't know why this bad omen keeps trailing me."

On the other hand, some people take up seemingly impossible tasks and face many challenges, yet they easily overcome them and achieve their desired results. Sometimes, a job stuck for a long time gets resolved miraculously. They are amazed at how it happened.

Actually, this is the play of our alignment with the divine vibration. Our thoughts and feelings affect our vibration, which causes us to be in tune with the divine vibration at times, and out of tune at other times. When we are in tune, we live in the feeling of "havingness."

Havingness is a new term that does not exist in the dictionary. It is the feeling of assurance of abundance, where there is unshakable faith in divine providence, no matter how the current situation appears. We attract and receive everything smoothly and easily. Otherwise, it is the reverse. The more we lack trust in the abundance of nature, the more we deprive ourselves of grace being showered on us.

What is this feeling of havingness?

Nature has everything in abundance; there is no scarcity. There is enough of everything for everyone. This is the unequivocal truth of life, yet people find it difficult to believe it. Many people focus on a lack in themselves, others around them, or the availability of adequate resources or favorable conditions. They wonder, "How can we live in a feeling of abundance when so many people in the world are struggling with scarcity and poverty? How can I succeed when I am bereft of the opportunities that others get? How can I be happy when I lack key qualities and skills?"

Consider a tree that bears abundant fruits. Even though it produces fruit in plenty, only those who go out and pick the fruit can enjoy it. The tree here is nature, and its fruit represents the abundance it provides. Going out to the tree and picking the fruit exemplifies action that emerges from the feeling of havingness. Those who shut themselves inside and complain of scarcity lack the feeling of havingness and cannot enjoy nature's abundance.

By holding onto limiting beliefs, we have created barriers preventing us from recognizing the abundance surrounding us. If we persist in holding onto thoughts like "No one loves me" or "No one respects me," we unknowingly block ourselves from receiving the love and respect already available. This is like holding an umbrella in the rain and complaining that there is no rainfall.

Similarly, people believe, "It is difficult to find a good Samaritan these days; you cannot trust anyone." Even if they long to have virtuous people in their lives, they will not find any because they have blocked such people out of their lives by holding onto this limiting belief.

There are many examples we pose as umbrellas that block the grace of nature's abundance from reaching us. For example, when we say things like, "Money doesn't last long with me," "Whenever I begin to feel better, I fall sick again," or "My friends and relatives always betray me," we are limiting our possibilities and creating barriers to the abundance that is available to us.

People usually change their thoughts and vibrations from scarcity to havingness only after they receive ample proof of providence, not before that. However, nature tells us, "Change your thoughts, start believing, and be in the feeling of havingness; you will receive everything automatically."

The limiting paradigm suggests, "You should first get what you want, then you'll feel assured, and then act." The havingness paradigm suggests, "First feel assured, actions will then emerge, and you will surely get what you want." When we start believing in the abundance of nature and change our tuning with understanding, the umbrella of wrong beliefs gets pulled down, and we begin to receive the shower of grace.

Nature is always ready to provide us with everything; we simply need to have faith in it. If we remain in harmony, love, peace, health, and prosperity, everything will fall into place automatically. At the same time, we must seek forgiveness for our feelings, thoughts, and actions that prevent us from receiving these blessings. This means all we have to do is remain aligned and feel, "This is it… everything is happening as per my divine plan… everything I need has been activated in my life," and leave the rest to nature.

How does the feeling of havingness work?

A lady could not conceive for many years despite undergoing various treatments. The doctors were also surprised and could not understand the reason. They inferred that everything was fine medically. Ideally, she should have conceived. So, what was missing that the doctors could not figure out? Medical science can treat only physical problems, not thoughts or emotions.

The problem was that the lady had created mental blocks due to her negative thoughts, which disturbed her alignment and prevented the joy of birthing from reaching her.

Let us examine what thoughts had taken root and continuously churned within her. In the past, the lady had experienced a miscarriage that created fear within her, leading her to believe that she would lose her baby again. Every time she was tested for pregnancy, she worried her test would be negative. She feared, "Even if I become pregnant, will I be able to give birth to the child? I doubt if I can ever be a mother. Maybe I am unlucky and not destined to be a mother."

With every passing day, she began harboring more negative thoughts about the child. Little did she realize that these thoughts had taken her away from the feeling of havingness. These thoughts hindered her chances of conceiving, and her vibrations created obstacles in her divine plan. If she were told, "You are unknowingly preventing the child from coming," she would not accept it and become angry, disturbing her alignment further. Thus, her thoughts of grief continued to increase.

Feeling exhausted, the lady eventually gave up and adopted a child. As soon as the child was brought home, she shifted to the feeling of havingness. Her thoughts changed, "I have a child. I am a mother now. I am experiencing the happiness of being a mother." As a result, her tuning improved, and she started feeling happy and content. Over time, she naturally conceived and gave birth to a healthy baby.

How did this happen? After a long period of trying to conceive without success, no sooner had she adopted a child than she naturally conceived and gave birth to a child. This happened because as soon as she became the adopted child's mother, all the mental blocks she had created dissolved. Thus, she removed the umbrella of limiting beliefs and aligned with nature opening the way to grace.

In other words, when we align our thoughts with the divine vibration, we remain in the feeling of havingness. This shift in our vibration opens us up to receiving everything.

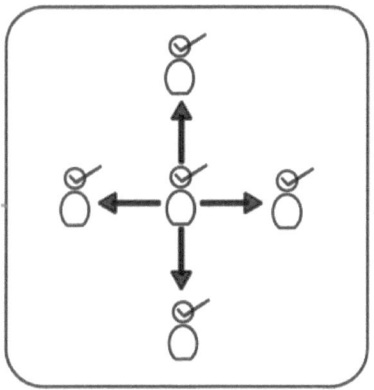

Be in the feeling of "Havingness"

Action plan:

1. Contemplate, what thoughts do you harbor more – abundance or lack?

2. Identify areas of your life where you feel a sense of lack, such as health, prosperity, relationships, success, beauty, intelligence, respect, etc. What aspects of life do you feel you have less or do not have at all?

3. Wherever you feel a lack, repeat the abundance mantra with complete conviction, "There is enough of everything for everyone, including me."

An Impersonal Life Boosts the Melody in Alignment

"There is no life greater than one dedicated to the well-being of all and no emotion greater than benevolence." All religious scriptures and great saints teach us this.

Leading an impersonal life is the easiest way to make our life harmonious, melodious, and attuned to the divine vibration. With this, we not only think and act well for our individual benefit but also the benefit of everyone else around us. However, after going through bitter experiences of the world, we presume that getting involved in others' concerns only causes us harm.

Then we become overwhelmed with questions like, "Should I think about myself first or others? What is the harm in living for ourselves? Why should we live for others? What benefit will it bring to us?" Let us understand the answers to all such questions through a story.

What to do for your own well-being?

A person had a large, beautiful garden with various fragrant flowers blooming all year round. He would sell those flowers in the wholesale market. There were many gardens around his garden, but his garden was the most beautiful and lush green; his sale was the highest.

However, he was still discontented because his flower production was more than his sale. Due to limited accessibility, few customers could reach him, and most of his floral yield would get spoilt and wasted, causing him losses. Moreover, the people around him were jealous of him. So, he had a poor relationship with them. Despite staying amid such a beautiful garden full of flowers, he was agitated for these reasons. None of the gardens in that area were at par with his because only his garden had an abundant natural water source. The other gardens could not get enough water to meet their requirement.

One day, to increase his earnings, he thought, "Why not start a lodge for travelers and increase my income." He opened a lodge with a few rooms and provided the best amenities for travelers to stay and also enjoy his garden. However, despite many efforts and advertisements, no one turned up. All his investment went to waste. One day, a traveler finally visited his lodge. He told the traveler, "Please tell others about this place, how beautiful the garden is, and how the fragrance of the flowers can be enjoyed throughout the day."

The traveler replied, "Indeed, your garden and these rooms are lovely, but all the other gardens around you are so dry and withered that no one feels like taking this route to reach your place. If the entire route and all the gardens en route become as beautiful as your garden, this place can become an ideal tourist destination. People will not just pass by this road but will want to stay here. If this area becomes famous, your lodge will run very well, and your flower business will flourish."

The person was convinced by this idea and thought, "He is right. If I want to prosper, everyone around me must also prosper." The following month, he laid an extended pipeline network to supply water from his reservoir to all the nearby gardens. By doing this, he not only ensured that he would not face a water shortage, but others also began to receive ample water. Slowly all the gardens flourished, and the place's fame spread far and wide. The area became known as the "Borough of Flowers." It was soon on the map of preferred tourist destinations that people from far-off places began to visit. Many flower merchants who used to buy and sell flowers in the wholesale market also began to visit the place in large numbers.

The person's lodge was always fully occupied. Other gardeners followed his example by building their lodges. Soon, the place became a famous tourist destination, and everyone flourished in their business and progressed further. All of them were very grateful to him, praised him, and held him in high esteem. Now, that person started living happily with his increased earnings and cordial and harmonious relationships with his neighbors. He had earned respect, prosperity, and everything he had ever dreamed of. His life had become harmonious.

He would often think, "Employing just one idea given by that traveler cost me nothing but look how I've gained because of that! Not only did I benefit, but others also benefitted. Hence, I must also work for others' well-being if I want my well-being. If only I had known this way of living earlier."

When we give, we do not lose but gain

People often read about benevolence and selfless living but do not believe in such a way of life because they do not understand the invisible laws of nature that govern life. Some think, "If we give something to someone, we will have less of it; we will lose it." But from this story, we have understood that by giving, we do not lose; instead, we gain multiples of whatever we give in return. If we want to achieve something, we should help others achieve it. We will see that it will come to us automatically.

If we want to progress in our career, we should become a catalyst for others' progress. If we want to be happy, we should become the reason for others' happiness. If we want to be loved, respected, and happily attended to, we should start doing the same for others. We will soon observe a change in people's behavior toward us. We will also receive love and respect and enjoy cordial relationships.

Conversely, if we cause someone sorrow, we will experience more sorrow. If we wish ill for someone, we will also experience it in our own life. It is a simple law of nature: Whatever we give to nature returns to us multiplied manifold.

In the story, the garden owner worked for the good of everyone, although in the process, he intended to do good for himself. But he was rewarded multifold. Imagine if our intentions behind benevolence were pure and selfless; what a miracle it would bring about! When our intentions are pure, we connect directly with the Source, align and tune with nature. Then the entire universe will shower its blessings on us.

A deep understanding of impersonal living

When we help others, we feel, "I am the one who is helping, and the other person is receiving help." However, this is an incomplete understanding that stems from a person-centric life. The correct understanding is, "The same Self – call it the Source, God, or Consciousness – is living through each of us. The living essence within each one of us is the same. Thus, the Source is helping itself through all beings. The one offering help is the Self, and the one receiving help is also the Self. All help is Self-help. There are no 'others.'"

The same Self is enacting the role of a helper through one body and that of a receiver through another. The Self is the doer and also the experiencer. As there is essentially no "other," one cannot do anything for someone else. With this understanding, we should lead a selfless, impersonal life. We should develop a firm conviction that whatever is done through our body is for God, not to fulfill any personal ambition. When there is no desire for personal gain, then alone can our actions be considered true service.

To lead an impersonal life or to render true service, we don't need to be physically present to serve someone. We can make our every emotion, prayer, thought, and action a form of true service, provided we use them as a means for the welfare of all beings, not just for our personal aims.

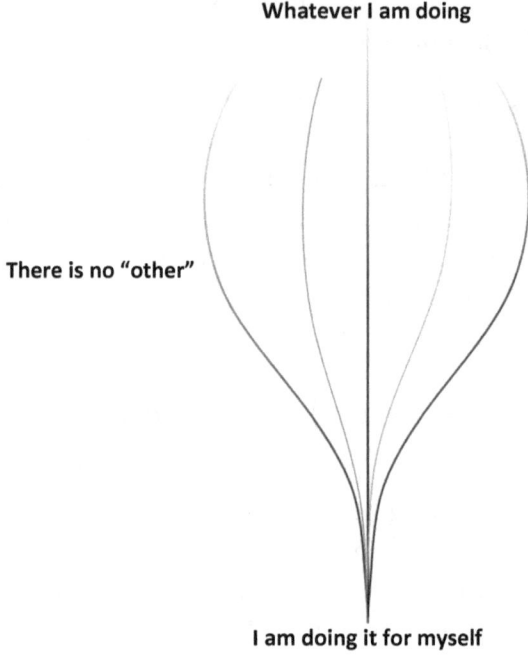

For example, a cab driver thinks, "I am doing this to earn a living. I will earn money from these trips. So, I must quickly drop off these passengers at their destination and pick up new ones." When focusing on personal gains, he may drive recklessly to reach early, honk excessively, and speak on the mobile phone while driving without bothering how the passengers feel. He is only concerned about himself.

Another driver thinks, "I am instrumental in taking my passengers to their destinations. Whoever rides in my vehicle should have a pleasant journey without inconvenience." As a result, he follows all the rules, drives carefully and peacefully, and does not honk unnecessarily.

So, by changing his mindset, the second driver's actions became a form of true service. Both drivers will earn money. However, the second driver converts his actions into service and experiences higher happiness, peace, and contentment, aligning himself melodiously. These emotions will also reflect in his behavior, and people will prefer to travel with him repeatedly.

Our vibrations reach people well before us. Everyone wants to work with positive, selfless people who are willing to go the extra mile. Such people never face any shortage of opportunities.

What to do in life now?

Whenever we talk about service or an impersonal life, our first thought usually revolves around feeding the poor, donating clothes to those in need, contributing to charitable organizations, or performing other kinds of service. However, service is not limited to these actions. As mentioned, service should permeate every aspect of our life, including feelings, thoughts, speech, and actions. We should always wish well for others, pray for them, and never speak ill of anyone. Our thoughts should always be positive with the betterment of all in mind. All our actions should be for the welfare of humankind, not just for any personal gain.

Last but not least, while rendering any service, our mind should never take any credit and think, "I have done this service." Otherwise, this feeling will inflate our ego and lead us away from the path of true service. Such thoughts disturb the mind and prevent us from fully aligning with the divine vibration. Therefore, we must avoid the egoistic feeling of being the doer and instead enjoy the bliss of impersonal life.

Action plan:

1. Contemplate the tasks that are held up in your life which you feel should have been completed. Also, contemplate how much you have helped others accomplish their incomplete tasks and contributed to their success. Can you help others selflessly without expecting anything in return?

2. Contemplate the underlying emotions that drive your actions, such as earning a livelihood for your family. Do you do it out of compulsion, selfish motives, or with the intention of give-and-take? Or do you do it with an attitude of selfless service?

3. Whatever work you do for your family or professionally, try to convert it into true service based on the understanding from this chapter. Perform every task with an attitude of service. Then observe what changes you experience in your life.

4. Perform an impersonal prayer for the well-being of everyone at any time during the day.

19

Fine Tuning with Divine Love

Love is inherently a divine quality. It is a pure and sacred feeling that revels in itself. Nothing needs to be added to it. Nothing can be taken away from it. It is not easy to express this feeling in words. But to understand it, let us divide it into "True love" and "Plastic love."

Plastic love is prevalent worldwide and is often mistaken as true love. So, let us first discuss plastic love.

Though plastic love contains the word "love," it is not love. It is like plastic flowers that appear real from a distance but are devoid of life, fragrance, and color. Plastic love is infested with longing, attachment, selfishness, restlessness, expectations, ego, insecurity, fear, doubt, comparison, jealousy, and lust.

When someone is attracted to another person, they may mistakenly believe they are in love. But attraction or infatuation is far from love. If they feel a sense of possessiveness or expectations for the other, such as, "He is mine," "She should do what I want," or "I will love him only if he loves me and keeps me happy," then where is the love? Like plastic flowers, this is fake love. It does not align us with the divine vibration but disturbs our alignment. It makes us selfish, insecure, egoistic, and restless.

The relationship between a mother and child is often considered the purest and most selfless form of love. Initially, when the child is tender, the mother feels unconditional love. But as the child grows up, the mother may begin to have unbridled expectations from him – "My child should excel like my neighbor's child," "He should always be by my side," "He should always agree with me," "He should marry the person of my choice," and "He should always obey me and not his partner." This is where the love begins to evaporate. The relationship that could have allowed the mother to experience the most profound love instead becomes the source of her sorrow.

The Indian epic Ramayana depicts this corruption of motherly love. Queen Kaikeyi ordained that her stepson Prince Rama, whom she loved dearly during his childhood, be banished from the kingdom for fourteen years to make way for her biological child, Bharat, to be crowned the king.

This selfish and plastic love always disrupts our alignment and prevents us from experiencing the bliss of true love. We cannot feel the unbroken, constant divine song of life within us and are shut to the divine guidance that is available within.

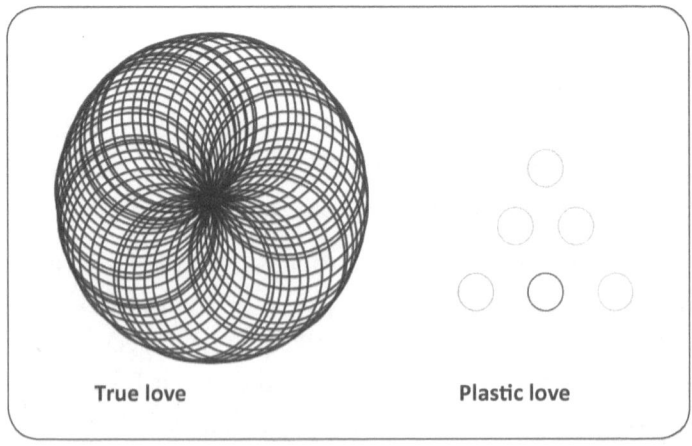

True love   Plastic love

The nature of true love

The peak of true love can be understood only when it is felt from the heart. Saint Kabir sings praises of true love in one of his couplets in the Avadhi language –

Pothi padhi padhi jag mua, pandit bhaya na koyi.

dhhai akshar prem ke, padhe so pandit hoye.

Many spend their lives reading and quoting the scriptures and die without wisdom. But the one who grasps the essence of the word "Love" enjoys the blissful union with true wisdom.

True love is characterized by being unconditional, steadfast, and devoid of attachment. It remains unchanged with time, situation, or circumstances and can never be too much or too less.

While some people may experience such love for a single person, the peak of true love is experienced when it overflows from the heart and radiates on everyone alike, without exception. Love then becomes the lens through which we see the world; we perceive everyone as the same divine consciousness that is our essence. This is devotion, the unconditional love felt for the presence of God in all of nature. At its peak, such love transcends worldly love, where the lover and the beloved become one.

In the Ramayana, Hanuman epitomizes true love. Similarly, Sri Ramakrishna Paramhansa exuded true love as he perceived the Mother Goddess within everyone. Whether a parent-child, husband-wife, siblings, friends, disciple-guru, or devotee-God relationship, true love is characterized by absolute surrender, lacks attachment, and is devoid of ego, making it pure love.

Saint Kabir has explained it in yet another beautiful couplet –

Prem pyala jo piye, shish dakshina dey.

Lobhi shish na de sake, naam prem ka ley.

One who drinks from the cup of love offers his head as an oblation unto God. The greedy never offer their head, though they keep bragging about being in love.

Here, the head symbolizes the ego. One who can surrender their ego alone can experience pure love. One who is greedy, attached, and unwilling to surrender the ego may speak eloquently of love but lack its actual experience.

True love always keeps us attuned to the divine vibration. Feeling such true love in the heart, a devotee always remains absorbed in listening to the eternal divine song of life, even while going through daily activities. As a result, their life is filled with bliss without any conflict, disturbance, or complaints of the mind.

The unconditional lover's tuning

The life of Saint Meera and Saint Chaitanya Mahaprabhu demonstrate the peak of unconditional love for God. From the worldly perspective, their state may be mistaken as a kind of madness, as they gave up everything in their love for Lord Krishna while expecting nothing in return. But only they knew the precious treasure they gained in their love for the Lord. They remained ever-attuned to Krishna Consciousness. There was indeed none as happy, fearless, or contented as them.

Unconditional love leads one on the path of liberation. It makes them fearless and allows them to let go of their desires happily and easily. Being absorbed in true love, they feel so content that they have nothing left to achieve; simply being in love is enough for them.

In contrast, with plastic love, people are always afraid of losing something, worried about preserving something, and lamenting about being separated from the object of their plastic love. Such love becomes the cause of bondage, not liberation.

True love is an inherent quality of our divine essence. It is our fundamental nature. Hence, we feel naturally inclined toward love. But out of habit, our comparing and judging mind contaminates the spirit of pure love with its beliefs, conditions, fixations, and tendencies.

One whose heart is not filled with love always feels an emptiness within. They try to fill this void by indulging in various relationships that serve the whims of their mind, but their heart remains empty and unfulfilled. Hence, they never feel fully satisfied all the time in any relationship. They always keep seeking something or the other to fill this void. This quest ends only when they start seeking true love. In this journey, the Guru acts as their guide and guardian to unite them with true love.

Action plan:

1. Reflect on your family and other relationships to determine which relationships are based on true love, plastic love, or driven by selfish motives.

2. With the understanding that "The same Consciousness that dwells in me is also living in them. They are also a part of the same divine Source," gradually awaken true love in your relationships that are currently based on plastic love or selfishness.

3. Having worked on the previous step, introspect what has changed within you. Have your relationships become happier, more peaceful, and harmonious? Do you feel more attuned to the divine vibration?

4. Contemplate, what kind of love do you feel for God? Is it based on the fulfillment of prayers? Is it based on a give-and-take attitude? Is it based on some fear, "If I do not love God, I will not receive divine protection, I will not succeed in my endeavors?" Or is it unconditional love? Are you God-loving or God-fearing?

5. Ask yourself, "Even if God does not fulfill my prayers, will I continue to love and worship Him?"

20

The Art of Staying Aligned

Have you observed the life of a great artist? They spend more time practicing their art than performing, whether they are musicians, singers, or sportsmen. Consistent and proper practice is crucial for them because, without it, they can descend from the pinnacle of success.

When we set a goal, we often pour all our energy, focus, and dedication into achieving it. We work tirelessly, day and night, pushing ourselves to the limit to ensure that we succeed. And when we finally reach that goal, we feel an overwhelming sense of satisfaction and accomplishment. But here's the thing: achieving success is only half the battle. The real challenge lies in sustaining that success over the long term. Without sustained effort and commitment, our hard-won achievements can quickly slip away, leaving us back where we started.

Similarly, attuning to the divine vibration and realizing the experience of the Self is one thing, and permanently stabilizing in that experience is another. Many seekers do attain the state of Self-realization but cannot remain established in that state for long. Due to a lack of consistent practice, understanding, or the arrogance of having attained the state of Self-realization, they often descend from that pinnacle of bliss.

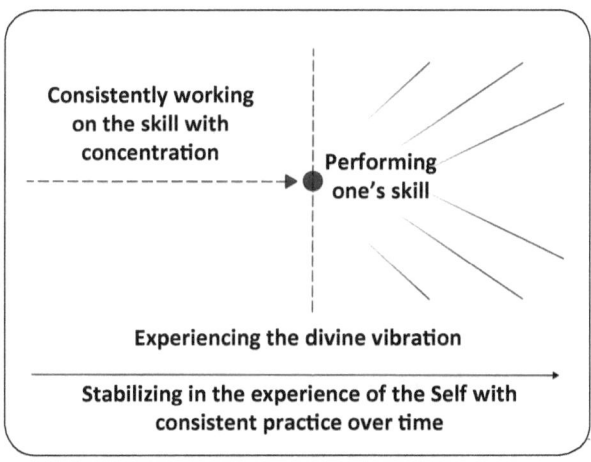

Given this, we must work to always stay aligned. If we are aligned today, we should continue to be aligned in the future. Just as sugar dissolves in water and becomes one with it, our alignment should become an integral fiber of our life and reflect in our feelings, thoughts, and behavior. Then, we will no longer need to consciously exert ourselves to stay aligned; it will happen automatically. We will breathe, speak, and act in alignment. Every feeling, thought, word we speak or write, and action will emanate from this state of alignment.

Hello, mic testing...

We have all attended staged shows, whether they were orchestras, plays, or speeches. Before the program starts, the microphone is tested. "Hello... Hello... test... test..." This checks whether the mic functions well and whether the audience can hear the voice properly.

This step needs to be done even before the main show. Even though the actual activity is the main event, this first step is equally important. If this step is not done well, all the work ahead could be spoiled.

Similarly, we must test our alignment before getting into action. If any misalignment is sensed, we must correct it first before starting the actual work. We need to check our alignment even if we are already aligned with the divine vibration. Before beginning any task or making any decision, we need to check our tuning. If we are attuned, all our work will be accomplished as desired.

Experiencing grace unconditionally

Dinesh Singh left his village in his youth and went abroad, where he earned a lot of money and fame, yet he was unhappy. He always felt a void within and always felt upset over trivial matters. Among the many causes for his sorrow and discontentment, the main reason was his leaving his homeland. He thought that he could be happier if he returned to his village.

One day, he left everything behind in the foreign land and returned to his village, where he met his childhood friend Jolly Singh. Jolly looked like a simpleton but had a decent livelihood. Dinesh felt pity upon seeing Jolly's financial condition. Although Jolly was not financially well off, his eyes radiated a strange spark.

Dinesh hesitantly asked him, "How are you doing, my friend?" He expected Jolly to complain about his hardships and commend him for having decided to go abroad, as there was nothing worthwhile left in the village.

But, on the contrary, Jolly said, "With God's grace and blessings, everything is going well." Dinesh was surprised. How could Jolly say everything was going well in such a miserable condition? He asked in astonishment, "Well, I don't see any such grace or blessings in your life."

Jolly replied, "What's bad here? Grace has constantly been showering on me. Although I do not have much work, I earn just enough to care for my family. We are a happy family. What more can I ask from God?" Jolly closed his eyes and thanked God.

Dinesh was taken aback upon hearing Jolly's response. He thought, "Even in these conditions, he can thank God and feel the grace. I had so much in life, yet why didn't I feel like this? I, too, was showered with so much grace, but I never felt grateful for it." For the first time in his life, he questioned his perspective as Jolly stood before him as the answer to his question.

Feeling God's grace, being grateful for it, and revering God, are not just meant to be expressed only when our desires are fulfilled. There will always be something that prevents us from being in gratitude. It could be some pre-condition – I can thank God only when this happens. It could be a shortcoming – How can I feel God's grace when He has not given me even this? It could be a reason – Why should I give credit to God when I have worked hard for it?

Feeling grace and being grateful are our inherent qualities. These qualities manifest when we recognize grace even in the most challenging situations. Regardless of our external circumstances, we can always find a reason to express gratitude and praise God. Even if we lose an eye, we can still be grateful that God spared the other. Whether there is a reason or not, gratitude can continue to flow.

The more we are attuned to the divine vibration, the more this quality will develop in us. And with daily practice of this quality, we will naturally remain attuned. The more we remain grateful, the more divinely aligned we will be.

Make gratitude a habit

In general, people tend to express gratitude when their desires are fulfilled. We need to ask ourselves, "If I get what I desire, whether it is a quality, talent, wealth, health, or anything else, will I be grateful? Will I be able to thank God for it?"

We may say, "Yes, of course, why not? I would surely express gratitude." Then we need to ask ourselves, "Have I ever expressed gratitude or felt thankful for all I have already received?"

Usually, we take what we have already received for granted and keep pursuing what we don't have. However, we need to be grateful to God for whatever we have already received. We need to cultivate the habit of being thankful by practicing it regularly.

Once we develop the habit of gratitude, it becomes easy to move ahead. We should also learn to be grateful for whatever we want but have not achieved. We should express our gratitude with the conviction that it will undoubtedly happen sooner than later because everything is in progress, even if it is not visible. God is working on it and will do what is best for us.

If we do not receive what we desire, we should understand that it is God's best choice for us. There is surely something better that God wishes for us. In any situation, we should express gratitude and make it a habit like Jolly Singh. If gratitude becomes an integral part of our nature, nothing can stop us from being free and happy. No power in the world can make us unhappy or disrupt our alignment!

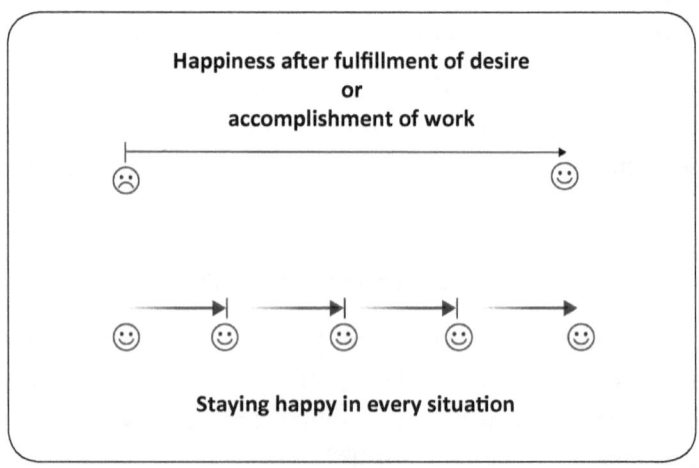

Shower compassion everywhere

Those who stay attuned to the divine vibration automatically start manifesting divine qualities. They always praise God, express gratitude, remain absorbed in devotion, and feel love and compassion for all. We often hear of many saints of yore whose sheer glance and presence would cure people's illnesses. People would start feeling better in their healing presence, get rid of their sinful ways, and start walking the path of devotion.

This is the power of a compassionate glance that radiates love, kindness, and equanimity for one and all. We should also have such a pure, divine gaze. We should make it a habit to spread only rays of love, compassion, and kindness with our gaze. Let our vision shower benevolence and auspicious feelings for everyone and bless whomever we see.

But what if the other person is so bad that, try as we might, we cannot feel compassion for them?

Firstly, we need to understand that we are not doing this as a favor to anyone but for our betterment. We should stay attuned to the divine vibration and awaken our divine nature. If we don't do this, we stand to lose first.

Secondly, we should always remember that the same Consciousness that dwells in us dwells in them too. Our gaze of compassion will help the Consciousness to awaken in the other person. We should contribute to this divine service. We should see the divine consciousness in others, not an individual persona. We should also thank God for choosing us for this divine service of awakening Consciousness. Imbued with a spirit of service, we need to glance at everyone with compassion.

By imbibing these divine qualities within and making them the very fabric of our nature, we will live in free flow. We will always remain attuned to the divine vibration. Leading life with ease, we will keep expressing gratitude and enjoy a life of liberation.

Agreement

I, ---------------------------(write your name here), on this date ----------in the presence of God (Divine vibration, Guru, nature) pledge that,

I will contemplate all the blessings bestowed on me and write them down. I will read them at least once daily and express my gratitude to God and nature.

I will also write down all the desires that have not yet been bestowed upon me, express my gratitude to God for those blessings, and have faith that these blessings will soon shower upon me.

Whomsoever I see during the day, whether people, animals, plants, trees, or anything in nature, I will shower them with love and benevolence through my gaze and pray for their well-being.

Signature

A Complete Flowchart of the Entire Book

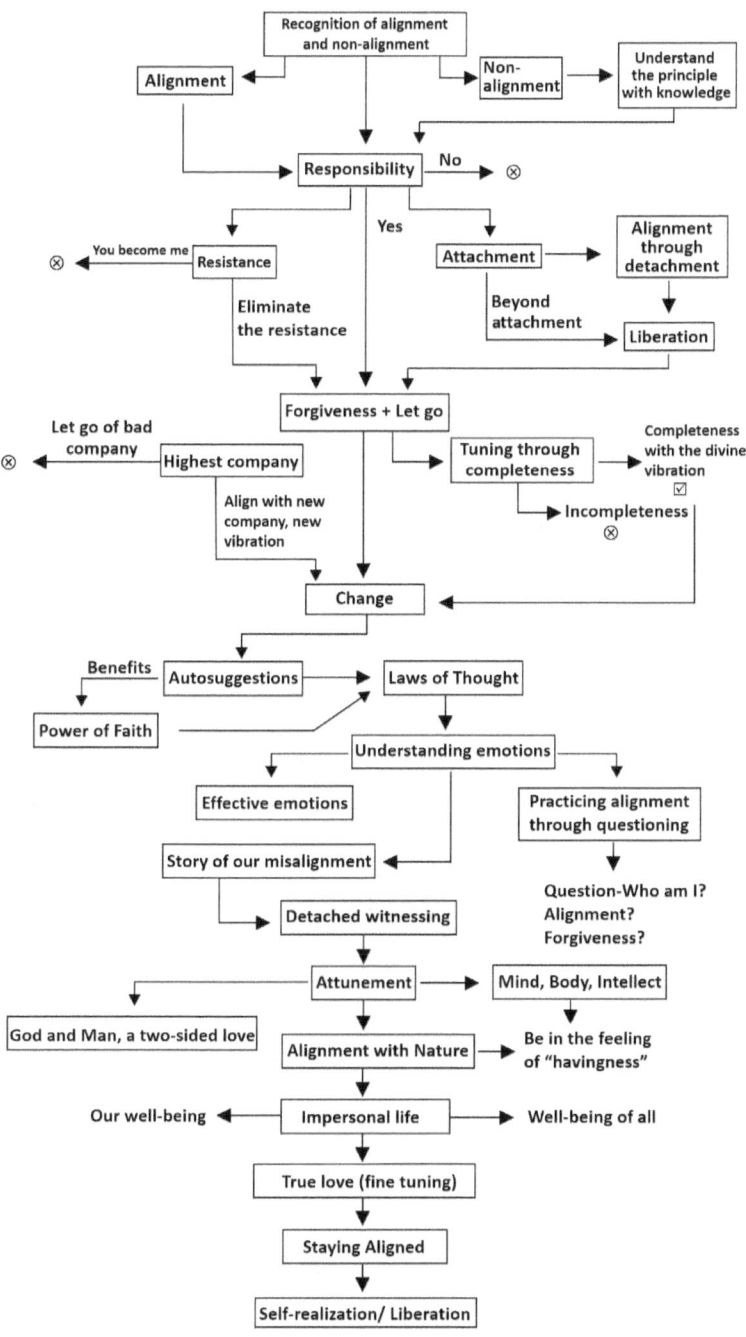

THE SECRET OF ALIGNMENT / 145

As you have read the entire book, you can enjoy the spiritual game of "Snakes and Ladders" in life. This book serves to indicate whether you are attuned to the divine vibration. If you have fallen out of alignment, this book serves to guide you toward getting back into divine alignment.

36	35	34	33	32	31
Self-experience	Art	Staying aligned	Ignorance	Guru	Divine love
25	26	27	28	29	30
Body	Nature	Presence / Havingness	Impersonal	Ego	Benevolence
24	23	22	21	20	19
Intellect	Mind	Alignment	Non-attunement	Questioning	Feelings
13	14	15	16	17	18
Incompleteness	Company	Vibration	Change	Auto suggestions	Laws of Thought
12	11	10	9	8	7
Completeness	Let go	Forgiveness	Attachment	Relations	Resistance
1	2	3	4	5	6
Beginning	Attunement	Laws of nature	Divine tune	Recognition	Responsibility

* * *

You can mail your opinion or feedback on this book to:
books.feedback@tejgyan.org

About Sirshree

Sirshree's spiritual quest, which began during his childhood, led him on a journey through various schools of philosophy and meditation practices. He studied a wide range of literature on mind science and spirituality. After a long period of deep contemplation on the truth of life, his quest culminated in attaining the ultimate truth.

Sirshree espouses, "All spiritual paths that lead to the truth begin differently but culminate at the same point – Understanding. This understanding is complete in itself. Listening to this understanding is enough to attain the Truth." Over the last two decades, he has dedicated his life to raise mass consciousness.

Sirshree has delivered more than 4000 discourses that throw light on this understanding. He has designed a system for wisdom, which makes it accessible to all. This system has inspired people from all walks of life to progress on their journey of the Truth. Thousands of seekers join in a virtual prayer for World Peace and Global Healing daily at 9:09 am and 9:09 pm.

About Tej Gyan Foundation

Tej Gyan Foundation is a non-profit organization founded on the teachings of Sirshree. The Foundation disseminates Tejgyan – the wisdom that guides one from self-development to Self-realization, leading towards Self-stabilization.

The Foundation's system for imparting wisdom has been assessed by international quality auditors and accredited with the ISO 9001:2015 certification. This wisdom has been presented in a simple, systematic, and practically applicable form that makes it accessible to people from all walks of life, regardless of religion, caste, social strata, country, or belief system.

The Foundation has centers in more than 400 cities and towns across India and other countries. The mission of Tej Gyan Foundation is to create a highly evolved society by leading seekers from negative thoughts to positive thoughts and further, from positive thoughts to Happy thoughts. A 'Happy thought' is the auspicious thought of being free from all thoughts, leading to the state of supreme bliss beyond thoughts.

If you seek such wisdom that leads you beyond mere knowledge, dissolves all problems, frees you from all limiting beliefs, reveals the true nature of divinity, and establishes you in the ultimate truth, then it is time to discover Tejgyan; it is time to rise above the mundane knowledge of words and experience Tejgyan!

The MahaAasmani Magic of Awakening Retreat

Self-development to Self-realization towards Self-stabilization

Do you wish to experience unconditional happiness that is not dependent on any reason? Happiness that is permanent and only increases with time? Do you wish to experience love, peace, self-belief, harmony in relationships, prosperity, and true contentment? Do you wish to progress in all facets of your life, viz. physical, mental, social, financial, and spiritual?

If you seek answers to these questions and are thirsty for the ultimate truth, then you are welcome to participate in the MahaAasmani Magic of Awakening retreat organized by Tej Gyan Foundation. This is the Foundation's flagship retreat based on the teachings of Sirshree.

The purpose of this retreat

The purpose of this retreat is that every human being should:

- Discover the answer to "Who am I" and "Why am I?" through direct experience and be established in ultimate bliss.
- Learn the art of living in the present, free from the burden of the past and the anxiety of the future.
- Acquire practical tools to help quieten the chattering mind and dissolve problems.
- Discover missing links in the practices of Meditation (*Dhyana*), Action (*Karma*), Wisdom (*Gyana*), and Devotion (*Bhakti*).

About Books by Sirshree

Sirshree's published work includes more than 150 book titles, some of which have been translated into more than 10 languages. His literature provides a profound reading on various topics of practical living and unravels the missing links in karma, wisdom, devotion, meditation, and consciousness.

His books have been published by leading publishing houses like Penguin, Hay House, Bloomsbury, Wisdom Tree, Jaico, etc. "The Source" book series, authored by Sirshree, has sold over 10 million copies. Various luminaries and celebrities like His Holiness the Dalai Lama, publishers Mr. Reid Tracy, Ms. Tami Simon and Yoga Master Dr. B. K. S. Iyengar have released Sirshree's books and lauded his work.

The Source
Attain Both, Inner Peace
and Worldly success

Awaken the Power of Faith
Discover the 7 Principles of the
Highest Power of the Universe

To order books authored by Sirshree, login to:

www.gethappythoughts.org

For further details, call: +91 9011013210

SELECT BOOKS AUTHORED BY SIRSHREE

   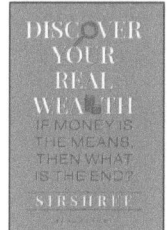

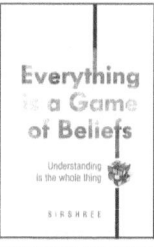   

To order these and other books authored by Sirshree
Visit **www.gethappythoughts.org**

Tej Gyan Foundation – Contact details

Registered Office:
Happy Thoughts Building, Vikrant Complex, Near Tapovan Mandir, Pimpri, Pune 411017, INDIA. Contact: +91 20-27411240, +91 20-27412576

MaNaN Ashram:
Survey No. 43, Sanas Nagar, Nandoshi Gaon, Kirkatwadi Phata, Off Sinhagad Road, Taluka Haveli, Pune district - 411024, INDIA. Contact: +91 992100 8060.

WORLD PEACE PRAYER

Divine Light of Love, Bliss, and Peace is Showering;

The Golden Light of Higher Consciousness is Rising;

All negativity on Earth is Dissolving;

Everyone is in Peace and Blissfully Shining;

O God, Gratitude for Everything!

Members of Tej Gyan Foundation have been offering this impersonal mass prayer for many years. Those who are happy can offer this prayer. Those feeling low or suffering from illness can receive healing with this prayer.

If you are feeling troubled or sick, please sit to receive the healing effect of this prayer. Visualize that the divine white healing light is being showered on earth through the prayers of thousands and is also reaching you, bringing you peace and good health. You can dwell in this feeling for some time and then offer your gratitude to those offering the prayer.

A Humble Appeal

More than a million peace lovers pray for World Peace and Global Healing every morning and evening at 9:09. Also, a prayer (in Hindi) to elevate consciousness is webcast every day on YouTube at 3:30 pm and 9:00 pm IST. Please participate in this noble endeavor.

www.ingramcontent.com/pod-product-compliance
Lightning Source LLC
LaVergne TN
LVHW041845070526
838199LV00045BA/1449